Looking for Home

Looking for Home

A Phenomenological Study of Home in the Classroom

෴

Carollyne Sinclaire

State University of New York Press

Published by
State University of New York Press, Albany

© 1994 State University of New York

For information, address State University of New York Press,
90 State Street, Suite 700, Albany NY 12207

Production by M. R. Mulholland
Marketing by Dana E. Yanulavich

Library of Congress Cataloging-in-Publication Data

Sinclaire, Carollyne, 1948-
    Looking for home : a phenomenological study of home in the
classroom / Carollyne Sinclaire.
        p.   cm.
    Includes bibliographical references (p.   ) and index.
    ISBN 0-7914-2039-6. — ISBN 0-7914-2040-X (pbk.)
    1. Classroom environment—United States. 2. Teacher-student
relationships—United States. 3. Phenomenology. 4. Interaction
analysis in education—United States. I. Title. II. Title:
Phenomenological study of home in the classroom.
LC210.5.S56 1994
371.1′023—dc20   93-37842
                                                                CIP
                                                                r93
                                                                Rev

10 9 8 7 6 5 4 3 2 1

≈

*To my mother and father
with love and thanks*

*and to my many teachers—
the children and students in my care
who shared their stories with me,
many of which are told within these pages:*

*Aaron, Adam, Allan, Amber, Amy, Andrea,
Bethany, Bianca, Bradley, Brent, Brian,
Brittany, Cassandra, Cristina, Danielle,
Deanna, Elizabeth, Emma, Evan, Francine,
Jenny, John, Josh, Judd, Kacey, Kristjana,
Leah, Lily, Mark, Matthew, Melisa, Michelle,
Nadine, Paul, Perry, Roey, Roland, Stephanie,
Sylvana, Tara, Theresa, Tim, Zachary;*

*to Elena, my student teacher, and to Mrs. Kaneko,
Mr. Koyama, Mrs. Nakaguchi, Mrs. Ohashi,
Mr. Okada, and Mr. Yamamoto in Japan.*

≈

Contents

Acknowledgments

I wish to thank Stephen Smith, for his unwavering patience, guidance and his push to "just write it"; Meguido Zola who told me I had a story to tell and badgered me to write it down; Ted Aoki for his suggestions, and Brenda McNeill for her meticulous reading of the drafts and her valuable criticisms.

Every effort has been made to clear permissions for world rights for the material in this book. However, in the event of any oversight, the publishers apologize and guarantee to make due acknowledgment or amendment in a subsequent reprint.

The editor and publisher make grateful acknowledgments for permission to reprint the following copyrighted material. Acknowledgments are made below.

Agee, James. "Knoxville: Summer 1915" reprinted by permission of Grosset & Dunlap from *A Death In the Family* by James Agee, copyright © 1957 by The James Agee Trust, copyright renewed © 1985 by Mia Agee.

Bollnow, Otto F. Reprinted from "Lived-Space" by Otto Bollnow in *Philosophy Today* (Vol. 5, Spring 1961). By permission of *Philosophy Today*. Copyright © 1961, *Philosophy Today*.

Bollnow, Otto F. Reprinted from "On Silence—Findings of Philosophico-Pedagogical Anthropology" by Otto Bollnow in *Universitas*, 1. By permission of *Universitas*. Copyright © 1982, *Universitas*.

Rylant, Cynthia. Reprinted from *Appalachia, the Voices of Sleeping Birds*, by Cynthia Rylant. By permission of Harcourt Brace & Company. Copyright © 1991 by Harcourt Brace Jovanovich.

Schutz, A. Reprinted from "The Stranger: An essay in social psychology" by A. Schutz in *Collected papers II: Studies in social theory*. By permission of Kluwer Academic Publishers. Copyright © 1964 Martinus Nijhoff.

Shaw, Stephen. Reprinted from "Returning Home" by Stephen Shaw in *Phenomenology and Pedagogy*, 8. By permission of *Phenomenology and Pedagogy*. Copyright © 1990, *Phenomenology and Pedagogy*.

Todd, Douglas. Reprinted from "Taoism: accepting life's flow in a hyper world" by Douglas Todd in *The Vancouver Sun*, (November 23, 1991). By permission of *The Vancouver Sun*. Copyright © 1991 *The Vancouver Sun*.

Vandenberg, D. Reprinted from "Openness: the pedagogic atmosphere" by Donald Vandenberg in *The Philosophy of Open Education*. ed. David Nyberg. By permission of Routledge & Kegan Paul. Copyright © 1975, Routledge & Kegan Paul.

van Manen, M. Reprinted from "Practicing Phenomenological Writing" by Max van Manen in *Phenomenology and Pedagogy*, 2. By permission of *Phenomenology and Pedagogy*. Copyright © 1984, *Phenomenology and Pedagogy*.

van Manen, M. Reprinted from "By the light of anecdote" by Max van Manen in *Phenomenology and Pedagogy*, 7. By permission of *Phenomenology and Pedagogy*. Copyright © 1989, *Phenomenology and Pedagogy*.

van Manen, M. Reprinted from *The Tact of Teaching*, by Max van Manen By permission of the State University of New York Press. Copyright © 1991, SUNY Press.

Introduction

Professor Meguido Zola, a writer of books for children, has worked closely with Carollyne Sinclaire, both in classrooms and at the university, for a number of years.

Meguido Zola: Can you capture for us, in a few words, what your book is about?

Carollyne Sinclaire: Well, let me give you a picture. Here we are, twenty-eight of us, all comfortably tucked into a corner of the classroom that serves as our reading circle: seventeen third graders, eleven fourth graders and me, their teacher. The soft and sometimes excited voices of children from other classrooms occasionally rise over our discussion and drift through the corridors of the school. I flip the page of the book to a story about a boy and his dog snuggled together under the bedcovers during a thunderstorm as the children huddle a little closer to the book for a better look. The story has a feeling of intimacy, boy and dog as cozy forces teaming against nature. When first reading it, the dog seems to be more frightened than the boy, but the children tell me the boy is consoling his dog for his own comfort.

I ask the children how they like this story compared to the nonfiction literature on dog care that we have been reading together and using to learn fact-gathering skills for note taking. Allan, a third grader, cocks his head to one side and says, "Well, **I** really like this story. The stuff about dog care is O.K. but. . . ."

Most students murmur their approval, nodding and agreeing. "Yeah, stories are **way** better. Better than nonfiction." They say this with conviction.

"Tell us about that, Allan," I say.

He continues. "Yeah, I like the stories better than the nonfiction. The facts in the dog care book are like talking **about** the thing. It's kind of like walking all around the thing from the outside. But when you read the story, it's different. The story is kind of like walking **inside** and talking from inside your heart."

In this book I want the reader to walk 'inside' my classroom to see the children, to hear their voices and to hear the "talking from inside [the] heart" of one teacher. The 'facts' in much of the literature about teaching are a "walk around the thing from the outside", that is, they talk about teaching from the outside . . . without entering into a real classroom. Unlike fiction, the stories in this book are true stories. Of course, the names of the children have been changed. These stories provide a walk into my classroom to penetrate the lives and thoughts and feelings of the children and the teacher.

M.Z.: What a wonderful image. So this is how you take

us inside your classroom . . . by telling stories?

C.S.: Yes, that's it. The book is composed of stories from my classroom and recollections and memories of my home from my own childhood, intertwined with discussion that ties the stories together. The stories focus on the day-to-day life in two of my classrooms, mainly over a three year period, with children from third to fifth grade. These children could be in anybody's class. When I come to share these stories with other teachers, they usually respond with, "Oh, that reminds me of . . . ," and then they begin to tell me a story from their classrooms.

M.Z.: Maybe you should tell us how you came to create this book . . . apart from the fact that we've all been badgering you to write down your stories.

C.S.: In a very roundabout manner. First of all, a group of teachers and teacher educators formed—people who were interested in telling stories from our classrooms. Sometimes we'd use children's books to act as a catalyst that might release stories for the telling. I found increasingly that when I told a story from the classroom, it would trigger a childhood memory for me.

M.Z.: Tell me more about the process.

C.S.: Well, the classroom incident would trigger a childhood memory for me. Those childhood memories—autobiographical stories—in fact, would remind me of the connection between the earlier events in my childhood and the way I am with children in the classroom today.

M.Z.: What did you want to do with the book?

C.S.: I wanted to portray the reality of the classroom and to understand the influences from my past that enable me to shape the environment for children. Rereading the classroom stories still didn't permit me to understand what I was doing in the classroom and why I was doing it that way; I was still "walking all around the thing from the outside." The childhood memories that surfaced during and after writing these classroom stories proved to be the key to unlock the relationship between past events and my present behavior in the classroom. These memories contain the principles that guide my practice and way of interacting with children.

M.Z.: So, you show the process happening in the book?

C.S.: Yes, the combination of the classroom stories linked with the memories allow me to portray one classroom reality by providing the children's voices—an account of what the children express—and to convey knowledge using my own voice—the teacher's voice—to share what I think, feel, experience and do. I wanted to make a connection with the teacher's thoughts and feelings from the past and tie that to present actions in the classroom with children. What I portray depends upon the meaning that I hold and interpret from the memories and classroom situations.

M.Z.: These stories give rise to universal themes, don't they? For instance: caring, relationship, risk, reliability, security, continuity, maturity and celebration.

C.S.: Yes, these themes are about how to make a classroom a place for intimate exchanges between teacher and students that help to make them both fully human.

M.Z.: And the overall idea you're trying to get at here is. . . .

C.S.:   . . . that we teachers should try to make our classrooms like home. 'Home', not just in the sense of the comfort of the second hand couch and chair, plants and private corners, but more.

M.Z.:   Yes, so true. . . . Tell us now about how you went about writing these stories.

C.S.:   Well, the kids would stream in the door in the morning with enthusiasms and concerns to discuss during morning sharing. That's an opportunity for them to raise concerns, ask questions, share joys and respond to others openly. I began to recognize the extraordinary qualities in the very ordinary moments in the day. Usually we had a silent writing time afterwards. As they were returning to their seats, I began frantically jotting down all I could: their actual words, gestures, when pauses occurred, moods. I wanted to capture all I could while it was fresh, often on napkins I had stuffed in my pockets from coffee in the staffroom.

M.Z.:   Well, you certainly have captured the feel of it. It's just like the third-grader Allan says, "It's like 'walking inside' the thing and listening from inside 'the heart' of the classroom."

C.S.:   I had to work very hard to listen. I went back often to the children to be sure that the language I wrote in was authentic. In my classroom we have a feedback time after silent writing in which the children read their works. At that time I would read them what I had written about our early morning sharing. Their reaction was one of incredulity at first, then some would become critical and determine the accuracy of the accounts. After one such reading, Aaron, my fifth grade student, said, "Ms. Sinclaire, the way you write it, it's true. It's just that it's almost more than true because you got right to the **important** stuff."

M.Z.: And how was it that you were able to have these discussions to reveal so much?

C.S.: I found that my admissions gave permission for the children to say more, to get to the heart of the matter, to hear how it was—from an older person, more mature and experienced, and their teacher. Together, we learned about each other.

M.Z.: So true. How did you get this kind of attunement to the children?

C.S.: Concentrating on writing at home and in the class helped me to listen better to the children. I kept sifting their words over as I wrote. There were many questions that arose for me: "What is it like to be a child in this classroom? What is it to be 'at home'? What is it to experience 'home'? What is it like to be 'at home' in the world? To be 'at home' in the classroom?"

M.Z.: This is so powerful. And I wonder . . . it must have affected your life. . . .

C.S.: Yes, a great deal. Understanding the origin of the influences of my commitment, what I do and do not do as a teacher, has had a transformational quality on my personal and professional life. I recognized the classroom to be my 'home', that place of intimacy, familiarity, and trust where I could create a place of ever-increasing openness in which children could grow. I wanted to create a classroom which could be a place for intimate exchanges; a 'home' for children. I wanted to prepare children to be 'at home' in the world. I recognized teaching to be my calling.

Sharing my writing and reflections opens up

the opportunity for me to have intimate conversations with my colleagues, the parents of my students, and my own family.

M.Z.: We often talk about becoming a community of learners. You must have found out some things about yourselves in this writing group.

C.S.: Yes, we discovered that we had similar experiences, rather like Ann Beattie's (1989) words from *Picturing Will*: "We are all so much alike, which is rarely remarked upon by artists." (p. 220) Our reactions upon finding this out were a sense of relief: we were not alone in our experiences any longer; and, at the same time, the grip of emotion the stories held over us was lessened by writing them down and sharing them with others. Through writing and discussion, I came to situate myself with others, amongst them, not apart. I found out what I had in common with others; as well, I discovered something of my uniqueness at the same time. I am not alone. The very act of writing, rewriting, and sharing it with members of the group places me in the midst of a community.

M.Z.: Now, you've titled the book *Looking for Home*. Tell us a little more about that—'home'. What does 'home' mean to you?

C.S.: For me, 'home' is a place which provides us with the sense of communion with others that helps the individual self emerge. Home helps us become conscious of the world around ourselves and establish an identity with others. Home calls to each of us as a search for the familiar, the intimate, the safe, the place where one can take risks, fail and be accepted back in.

M.Z.: Yes. Is creating home in the classroom some-

thing that more of us, as teachers, should do? Is
this why you're writing this book?

C.S.:   Yes, all of those things. In order to know what
we want to do in our work with children, where
we want to lead them, and towards what end we
endeavour to reach jointly, beyond that of merely
the mandated curriculum, we teachers need to
know ourselves, who we are, and how we came to
be that way. I was not aware of these influences
before I began to unravel the events of my childhood. But in writing these autobiographical
pieces, I alone bear the responsibility for my own
story.

As the teacher and the author I possess
many advantages here, for I hold the power of
the storyteller, and in the telling, the power to
give meaning to the event. At the same time,
through the stories and admissions, I have
exposed myself and leave myself vulnerable to
judgment. Publication of these classroom stories
and my own embedded memories could mean
opening the door to accountability, differences
of values, and criticism from many sources:
parents, teachers, counsellors, university faculty.
I'm not trying to revise history; instead I'm trying
to recapture from my memory some of the attitudes we had in the fifties. I might have chosen
to keep the pieces as a journal that would serve
to inform only me and, in doing so, I would have
chosen isolation over defending my sense of self.
But isolation is a form of denial of self.

M.Z.:   Then, what is the reward for telling your stories?

C.S.:   The work has allowed me to affirm some of my
practices. It has permitted me to forgive and
learn from some of my mistakes. It has empow-

ered me to evolve my self through my teaching. In writing the book, I penetrate and "walk inside" to "talk from inside my heart", to hear my own voice and to be heard. This, to me, is being 'at home'.

1

Looking for Home

Souvenir from Home

"As I pass a balloon to each one of you, you will feel the tug of the string as it gently lifts you up, higher and higher, until you are floating gently, safely out of this room." I hear the professor's voice as I give in to her guided visualization at a summer workshop on 'Differentiating Curriculum for the Gifted'. We are taking part in a strategy we could use in our classrooms with kids.

"Choose your favourite color and see it, a new balloon . . . yours," she says. It makes a squeaky latex sound as I run one hand over its red newness. Eyes closed, steady breathing, body more relaxed than I can remember, I am transported to lightness and freedom.

"Feel your balloon lift you out of the theatre, each one of you floating down the hall and out the opened doors. See your companions, wave to them, as the distance grows greater between you and them."

The pauses in the professor's speech allow me to take in each image. Huge, fat Ruth seated beside me, lifts up and away effortlessly. Joy takes over her rippling face and the sound of the wind replaces her constant chatter. I feel the warmth of the sun on my back.

"Everything's okay . . . you are safe . . . this ride is yours. Float higher and higher." Far below me the university shrinks. I scan the expanse of sandy beaches; waders and sandcastle builders are specks below. "You're going to travel back in time, back to the time when you were a child." In flight, I'm not conscious of my body as I drift softly, warm and serene.

"You're going back to your neighbourhood, the place where you grew up. Perhaps for you there were many places. Choose the one that has significance," the instructor says. I am hardly aware of the multiple choices for some because I grew up secure in one house. I hover weightless above the hill I used to coast down on my bicycle as a child, wild hair flying, free—gypsy girl. I soar above the dump I rooted in, where I discovered the deer's head, its eyes glazed over, antlers removed. The rubble remains heaped despite the later arrival of the bulldozers of the late fifties, the cement mixers, the moving vans, that changed our 'playground' forever. I hover over Frew's Grocery where I lined up for penny candy, breathless in the hope that the sugar strawberries wouldn't be gone by the time I got to the front of the line. And polite always, for Mrs. Frew had a bad temper with the wavering indecision of children. I linger awhile over Rosalind Jung's backyard where we played tents and Arabs. Then I drop down to peer in the kitchen window where her mom made jokes in Chinese and whacked meat with a cleaver. I slow down to look closer at the lilac bush under which I buried Fluffy, my cat, in the shoebox. That same lilac bush later provided cover for Caroline Harrison and me, the two 'Carolines', to hide in the tall grass and watch the 'Eye-talians' move in while we whistled at them with blades of grass stretched taut between our thumbs. As children, we tried to decide if they were really 'white people'.

"Feel the balloon gently descend. You are on the street in front of your home. See the place you grew up in. See the door and take your time walking up to it. Enter the same way you did as a child," she continues.

I feel cold suddenly. Is the wind whipping up the street off the mountains? I hesitate to approach my door, although I've never felt that way or had reason to before. I let my feelings take over and an anxiety tightens up my muscles. The front yard is so bare—those monkey trees never took and the ground looks so parched. Hydrangeas, how I hate them. Not blue, not pink, not purple. In our yard, the mottled mixture of neglect. Oh! The house is smaller than I remember it.

I press down the latch, and with the same give as before, the door opens. I step in. Sun streams in through the windows, past venetian blinds and crisscrossed curtains, to form a solid shaft of light in which cigarette smoke and dust particles hang. A still, golden glow suspends over the rooms. There is a smell of dust.

A large, curved arch delineates the living room from the kitchen. There's the old wood stove where I made my potions—mixtures of spices I would boil on the burners in a small iron frying pan. I used the 'stinks', as I called them, to create incantations that would drive out imaginary devils in front of the open burners. I'd seen natives doing it in fifties B-movies. From the ceiling hangs the rack where my father used to hang his union suit to dry in winter, every stain on display. Then I see the gas stove which replaced the early wood model. Images and eras flicker in and out but the golden light continues to cast its dim shadow over the past.

"See the people who lived there. Your family. Others. See them as they were, doing what they did," the professor leads and I follow.

I call out, "I'm home," but my family doesn't hear me. No one responds. Strange. My father is in the living room where the television takes preeminence over everything else. His face is to the plaster wall, his back to me, his tool kit at his side. "Dad, dad!" I shout, wanting his attention. "I'm home. . . ."

My voice is feebler as I catch on to the idea that they don't hear me. My brother is posted at the back door wearing his grey melton cloth jacket with its pocket torn off by firecrackers lit and stuffed inside. He's probably looking for his friends, ready to make a swift exit. But he, too, is motionless. They all are, as though they are mock ups of themselves from the past. My mother's lean back is tethered by apron strings as it faces me. She is in the nook surrounded by flour and sugar in yellowing buff canisters with red lids. The nook is hers, a place where my mother rolled out pie crust, and fluted swags and roses, all ornamental stuff to fill up her life. But there is no motion now, just stillness. "If I call out, she won't answer me either," I think. "I won't bother."

I wander the house becoming the child I was, entering into the stillness. It's not quiet, though. There is the familiar hum of the Frigidaire and the reliable creak of a few floor joists. Nobody's seen me and I might be disturbing them, so I tiptoe as I always did, never loudly, not on my heels. Until this time, I'm unaware of my sadness at not being "seen" and at not receiving a welcome.

In the solitude of the hallway I am shocked by my desires for the first time: to be hugged, to be rushed at by my family, to be surrounded, thronged and brought in close, to be at the center. To be cherished and listened to, without judgment. I begin to cry as I continue down the hallway to the addition. I walk past the scary part, where the stairs divide into basement and bedrooms. This is where my grannie's ghost came to live after she died.

"Enter your room, the room where you slept, where you kept your things and find a meaningful object. The layer of wallpaper I chose as a teenager peels away. The riotous crazy-quilt pattern exceeded my cheeriness at that age. The room is restored to the pink of my childhood. It's nearly empty except for a chenille bed cover, a plywood desk my dad made, and a chest of drawers. I always called them 'chesterdrawers' to match the term, 'chesterfield'. My tears handicap my frantic search in the closet for a meaningful souvenir—the upside down mammy doll, the copy of *Charlotte's Web* I won from a t.v. program, my faded sewing kit. I hold them up one by one and appraise each item, but none has any special significance. I rifle the drawers—nothing. I'm blinded by a mixture of mascara and tears; my nose is running and I'm obsessed with clutching at the past for something I can't find, and stunned by something I've discovered.

"It's time to go back. You leave the house behind, closing it up the way you came in. It was just a visit. You can go back any time. But now your balloon is lifting you up," reminds the professor.

My time is up and I am empty handed! I lift off the ground, sobbing. A hand reaches across and presses a wad of tissues into mine. . . .

There must be more images about landing but I miss them all. I blow and wipe as quietly as I can.

"Just relax. Take your time. Come back to the room whenever you're ready."

The workshop leader comes close to me and whispers, "I didn't say anything or stop because I thought you could handle it." I nod, wincing, holding back the pain.

The Desire to Return Home

My family lived in separate solitudes, each of us: my mom, my dad, my brother, and I. Everyone went his or her own way. I don't remember us connecting with each other in intimate ways. We talked about things, daily events, but they were facts, stripped of feelings. If I asked my dad for advice or told him my troubles, he'd snap at me, "Don't tell **me** your troubles. I've got troubles of my own." Then he'd turn to his tool bag and prepare to leave for work.

If talk wavered over the edge into an area that might "upset someone" the conversation was stopped. "That's not pretty," my father would say.

Or: "You don't feel that way. No, you don't," my mother assured me. She couldn't bear for me to feel that way. So I couldn't feel that way. It was wrong to feel that way. So I didn't, not outwardly. I just didn't say. I held my **feelings** in secret. And some I denied and buried deep inside me until this visualization.

The guided visualization of the professor encouraged me to experience the feelings about home as it was in another time. Taking part in the visualizations helped me to discover certain truths about my home. My home was not 'home' in the sense of letting down one's hair, a place where one could have rest and refuge. It was a place where we conformed to strict guidelines that excluded baring our souls.

Prior to the visualization I had often romanticized returning home. I felt a need to capture something that might have been; to grasp once again something I considered to have been satisfying, free of problems. But my memory of home was something elusive which had "mutated with age." (Shaw, S., 1990, p. 226). Still I felt a need 'to return' in my mind to a home where I felt more secure, more protected, and more at peace with the world and myself. The urge to return home is explained by Stephen Shaw (1990):

Perhaps it is one way in which we strive to fend off the darker and more stressful moments of our lives, to cling to a knowledge of hope that our lives will return to a more ordered and positive setting where we will be able to grow once more and experience the satisfaction of acknowledging that growth, and in many unobtrusive ways having it acknowledged externally.

For almost everyone the notion of home is usually a positive one. It is the known as opposed to the unknown; it is certainty as opposed to uncertainty, security rather than insecurity, the knowledge that in the final analysis someone else, our parents, will make the necessary decisions and will protect us from harm. It is the familiar and predictable. Better that than the unknown, the unpredictable, with a stranger imposing strange ways. It is also the primordial sense of the need for security, of being held, of belonging. (p. 226)

My personal conscious search for 'home', stemming from the visualization I had taken part in the year before, enhanced my desire to create 'home' in the classroom. This was evident in the increased sensitivity I demonstrated towards my students over the next year. I was at a point in my teaching career where I had become comfortable with curriculum and instruction, and I began to put an increasing emphasis on the children themselves. I was asking myself, "What would it be like to be a child in this classroom? To be doing these activities? To be with others in this classroom?" I was working towards making my classroom a more personal place to be, not just cozy in the sense of the physical environment, but in the way that children interacted with each other.

As a learner and a reader, I noticed more books, articles and short stories with titles and themes that dealt with home. I found images of home in literature as I read and connected those images to my own memories. I began to write my childhood memories, and as I read and reread them, the experience reminded me of that described by Robert Frost in his poem "Ghost House" (Lathem, 1969):

> I dwell in a lonely house I know
> That vanished many a summer ago,
> I dwell with a strangely aching heart
> In that vanished abode there far apart. (p. 6)

It was painful for me to "dwell" on home because of the contrast between my romanticized, superficial recollections in the past and those memories I repossessed through the concentration of writing and reexamining them. What had vanished were the concrete exterior images of recollection, and I found myself inside the core of feelings of moments from long ago.

There were many images from literature that helped me clarify my own ideas and feelings about my desire to 'return home'. Robert Frost, in his poem "The Hired Man" (Lathem, 1969, p. 38), creates a dialogue between a farmer and his wife, the subject of which is the return to the farm, in the farmer's absence, of a somewhat unreliable and lazy old labourer who is now ill. In the past, the hired man has not really done a day's work for a day's wages. After a lengthy discussion with his wife, the farmer refuses to give in to her pleas to rehire him and maintains his own resolve. The farmer goes inside the house to tell the man his decision. On reaching the hired man's bedside, the farmer finds that the labourer has died in his sleep. During the dialogue the wife says, "Warren . . . he has come home to die".

>"Home is the place where, when you have
>   to go there,
>They have to take you in."
>"I should have called it
>Something you somehow haven't to deserve." (p. 38)

I shared with Frost's hired man a need to return to that same sense of security, the familiar, the predictable and the belonging. From the poem I learn that 'home' does not have to mean the place in which we were born or where we lived with our families; it is defined by something else. Nor is home a place which we have to earn, as Shaw (1990) points out:

>It does not matter what you have or have not done, there is always a place for you at home. This implies the idea of acceptance, an understanding by another that this is also your place of being and that in it you simply are. (p. 232)

I discover an added but complementary meaning in Schutz's "The Homecomer", in which he refers to home as a "starting point and a terminus" in the lifetime journey of an individual (1971, pp. 107-108). Home, then, could be that place where our journey into the world begins and ends. Home is "the point or place in which we feel secure enough to begin taking risks and from which we embark on adventures"; home is the place "to which we return triumphant or discouraged." (Shaw, 1990, p. 232) As Frost's hired man goes home to die, I am reminded that home holds more than just a geographical place in our lives.

"Home is where we are born or at least become conscious of the world and first establish identity in relation to others." Home is a "notion" (Shaw, 1990, p. 232). "The symbolic character of the notion 'home' is emotionally evocative and hard to describe" says Schutz (1971) who points out the possibility of individual interpretations:

> . . . home means one thing to the man who has never left it, another thing to the man who lives far from it, and still another to him who returns . . . [it] is an expression of the highest degree of familiarity and intimacy. (Schutz, 1971, pp. 107-108)

Home is defined in different ways depending on who we are; though what we all have in common in our personal definition of home is the familiarity and intimacy found in relationships.

When we examine the root of the word home we see that the need for security is universal. The first appearance of home in the Indo-European base form is "kei", meaning to lie or settle down. This is related to the German to lull or put to sleep. In Old Norse the word "heimr" means residence or world. The Old Irish word "doim" or "coem" derives from the same root and means dear or beloved (Webster's, 1969).

Home, then, is that which provides us with the sense of communion with others that helps the individual self emerge. Home helps us become conscious of the world around ourselves and establish an identity with others. James Agee's "Knoxville: Summer 1915" (1983) renders the atmosphere of communion as a comfortable intimacy found by a child with his family:

> On the rough wet grass of the back yard my father and mother have spread quilts. We all lie there, my

mother, my father, my uncle, my aunt, and I too am lying there. First we were sitting up, then one of us lay down, and then we all lay down, on our stomachs, or on our sides, or on our backs, and they have kept on talking. They are not talking much, and the talk is quiet, of nothing in particular, of nothing at all in particular; of nothing at all. The stars are wide and alive, they seem each like a smile of great sweetness, and they seem very near. All my people are larger bodies than mine, quiet, with voices gentle and meaningless like the voices of sleeping birds. . . ." (p. 7.)

It is interesting that in Agee's picture the family is "lying down" or "settled"; they are amongst their "beloved"; and they are in silent "communion" with each other. The passage includes the physical and emotional attributes found in the etymology of home.

The Call of 'Home'

Home has the quality of 'otherness' even when the other is absent. The feeling can be portable, a reminder of the familiarity shared when the other is near. Michael J. Rosen (1992) describes this feeling in his introduction to the children's book of poems entitled, *Home*:

Home is like what you take away each time you leave the house. Like a wristwatch, it ticks beside the ticking that is your heart. Whether or not you hear it, look at its face, or feel its hold, We're with you is what the minute, hour, and second hands of home have to tell.

Home is the place that goes where you go, yet it welcomes you upon your return. Like a dog overjoyed at the door, We've missed you is what you hear, no matter how long you've been gone. (p. 3)

The concrete objects of home evoke a sense of the familiar and the intimate as pointed out by the idiomatic phrase: "There is a little bit of home in this. We bring things from home to put up around us in the new abode because in the things themselves there is the space of home." (Winning, 1990, pp. 247-248) Heidegger speaks of the objects from home in relation to one's own home: "Even when we relate ourselves to those things that are not in our immediate reach, we are staying with the things themselves." (1964, p. 334) Things from home evoke a feeling, as Michael J. Rosen (1992) points out:

Home is all the things you know by name: a family of dishes, books, and clothes that waits for you to choose among them every day. We're ready for you is what the chorus in your house sings. Your finger-prints are grinning on their faces (p. 3).

In my guided visualization I was able to remember the things from my childhood that were so familiar and evoked the memories of my home, but when the time came to choose something with special meaning, none of these objects symbolised the intimate quality of home I look for. At that point in the visualization I became more desperate in my search.

Rosen (1992) points out that it is the familiarity and intimacy of 'other' that helps to etch out the uniqueness of the individual: "And home is all the names that know you, the one and only person who does just what you do." (p. 3)

Home calls to us: it reminds us of home when we are away, "We're with you"; it calls us in, "We've missed you"; it welcomes us in, "We're ready for you". Home calls to us to be part of a community: "Home is all the words that call you in for dinner, over to help, into a hug, out of a dream." (Rosen, 1992, p. 3) Home calls to each of us as a search for the familiar, the intimate, the safe, the place where one can take risks, fail and be accepted back in:

> Come in, come in, wherever you've been. . . .
> This is the poem in which you're a part.
> This is the home that knows you by heart.
> (Rosen, 1992, p. 3)

Because the call of home is as unique to the individual as is the definition of home, it is difficult to explain to someone else. In her picture book, *Appalachia* (1991), Cynthia Rylant describes it thus:

> Those who do go off, who find some way to become doctors or teachers, nearly always come back to the part of Appalachia where they grew up. They're never good at explaining why. Some will say they had brothers and sisters still here and they missed them. But most will shake their heads and have a look on their faces like the look you see on dogs who wander home after being lost for a couple weeks and who search out that corner of the yard they knew they had to find again before they could get a good sleep. (p. 5)

I ask myself, then, what is that calling for home for me if it is not to be found in my memories of my own home? And where is my home, then, if it is not the home in which I grew up? Can I find that sense of home for my soul somewhere else? I have felt the calling of teaching—a pedagogical calling—and I have responded to the 'calling' of a child who is in need of care. Max van Manen (1991) reminds me that "the pedagogical calling is that which calls, summons us to listen to the child's needs" and draws child and parent—in this case, child and teacher—"into oneness." (p. 25) This pedagogical calling has been a quest for me, with similarities to the one I embarked upon in the guided visualization to find a symbolic object, a reason for my journey.

I believe that the next story may be the beginning of my quest for a home for my soul, when, as a teenager working part-time in a cafeteria, I am given advice by the senior bus girl to "do something that lasts." That "something" would allow me to settle down and reside or "dwell" in the "strong sense of watching over something, preserving a space where the human being can feel sheltered, protected", much like the "idea of a house with its wall and fences [as] a "safe keeping" . . . "of something which needs to be watched over." (van Manen, 1984, p. 54) Instead of a "house with its wall and fences", my "house" would be my classroom, and my "home" a space of intimacy for myself and my students there within. I would learn to "dwell" in the classroom as a teacher, in which I would realize my "true essence." (Bollnow, 1961, p. 33)

Searching for Home

Do you remember the White Lunch Cafeteria on Granville Street? The one with the neon sign with the people circling holding a tray. The manager phoned, "You applied for a part-time job as a bus girl? If you want it, come in on Friday and get your uniform and training." He hurled his words at me, "You want it?"

I couldn't hide my enthusiasm. "Oh, yes. Thank you. Eighty-five cents an hour? This Friday, that's this Friday the 19th? Quarter to five. Oh, thanks." My first job—bus girl.

My uniform was black and rustled when I walked. It was intended to fit someone else—princess lines with a bust that curved lower and larger than mine. "Walk fast dear, no one will notice," Louise told me. She was the senior bus girl, the one who wore a cap with a stripe, in charge of training all of us on the floor. Louise was no girl, though. She must have been in her seventies. Rez capsules tinted more of her scalp than her hair and her eyesight betrayed her at the mirror, leaving a dotty spackle of Maybelline on her withered cheeks.

"You're just part-time, aren'tcha?" Louise squinted at me out of one eye as she folded her wiping rag carefully on the handle of her cart. "You're just stayin' for the summer, though? You're not gonna quit school for this, are ya?" she badgered. "Okay, that's better. 'Cause this is no job to make a livin' at." Louise backed the cart out of the station, automatically filling it with vinegar shakers, white and malt, loading on plastic dispensers with the words 'Ketchup' and 'Mustard' written in gold letters on their sides. "Come along with me and I'll show ya the ropes, then."

"Look at me, at my age, workin' at this. I never got a good education. You stay in school, ya hear me." Her bent body wheels around and she peers at me, hunched over the table, waiting for my agreement. I nod; she intimidates me.

"All I ever wanted was to do somethin' that would stay put. Somethin' that would last. Look at me! Here, I clean up dishes and I wipe. All day I wipe. They come along, eat and mess it up all over again. I come back and I have to wipe up again." She moves close to me and studies my face, whispering in confidence so management won't hear, "It never lasts."

"Mmhmm," I nod, as though I understand.

"You get a good education. You get a good job," she lectures me in secret from behind a fist closed on a wiping rag that smells of ketchup and ashtrays: "Do something that lasts."

Throughout the years since, in the many jobs I held, I have thought of Louise's words. They haunted me when I worked in mind-dulling office jobs where the only measure of my value as a person was the number of keystrokes per hour I could perform. I wanted something more lasting at the end of the day than the heap of card chips that filled up my machine. Louise's words had become my crucible.

Later, even as a student teacher, I sought help from my sponsor teacher, and she replied, "Yes, you taught them that yesterday. But you'll have to teach them that again. They forget—they're kids."

I railed to myself, undermining all my efforts, "I thought this was something important, something that would have an effect!" Twenty-five years after Louise taught me how to wipe out ashtrays, I erase a lesson on the chalkboard at the end of the day and I reflect on her words. I think of a phone call I received last week.

"Hello, Carollyne? It's Beth, . . . from Grade five . . . from Sunnyview." It's Bethany who was in my class two years ago, the sort of girl who bursts with uncontrollable enthusiasm, the kind you want to take aside and tell the facts of life before they happen to her.

"You know Deanna? You remember? She's smoking, and you know what else?" her voice turns to a whisper as she turns her best friend in, "She's making out. Ummhmmm." "No, I'm not. Not me. My mom would kill me." "And Brian, he failed every subject and he doesn't even care. Tim, he came back, but he's a snob. No one will even talk to him." Bethany tells me about **everyone** we both knew. She rebuilds every bridge between us, me, as I am now, teacher of city children, and her former confidante, ally and teacher in what the principal called, "a school of biker dads and born-again parents."

Bethany hesitates on the phone. She is holding back something that is the very reason for her call. Her voice becomes that of a nine-year old, "I still have all my poems. The ones I wrote with you." That was the year Bethany told a family secret that she had held in her heart for many years. My friend and colleague and I organized a writer's conference for the children to share their works. The reporter from the local paper came, moms poured in the door; even a school official showed up.

When it came Bethany's turn, she stepped up to the microphone and calmly read a poem she wrote to her cousin who had drowned four years before. She spoke to that child, telling her she would not be forgotten, and that she was still loved. She shared her longings with an audience of strangers while her mother sobbed quietly into hankies offered by other moms seated at her side in the back row of our classroom. Beth spoke the words a family could not say; she expressed the feelings they had hidden from each other.

"And you know what?" Bethany says, her confidence building, "I wrote a song and I'm gonna get it published." I smile as I wipe away today's chalk, all the while thinking of Bethany. On second thought, I wonder if there is, indeed, a job with effects that last longer than teaching.

I had been looking for a meaningful objective, to "do something that lasts." Bethany's words reassured me that I was in possession of the object of my quest. I was answering the calling of teaching that would allow me to settle down, to reside, to dwell—to realize my true essence—to be 'at home'. Later I would recognize the classroom as 'home', a place of intimacy, familiarity and trust where I could create a place of ever-increasing openness in which children could grow. A child's family home does not always permit him or her to speak from the heart. Bethany was able to find that freedom and safety to speak out in the classroom. In her family, the cousin's death had been an emotion-filled unspoken subject, which had become a taboo topic. But the right classroom can be a place for such intimate exchanges, a 'home' for children.

What does it mean to be 'at home'? Can one be 'at home' outside of one's own house? These are questions I grapple with in the classroom, and I begin to understand as I read Otto Bollnow's (1961) 'Lived-Space' in which he outlines the difference between "house" and "home". He asks the following questions about 'home': "But after I have returned to my place of residence, am I really 'at home' there? Where is my real home?" (p. 32). Bollnow refers to a person's house as a "reference point from which [that person] builds his [or her] spatial world" (pp. 32-33). But the author points out that it would be an exaggeration to call the individual house the center of a person's space (pp. 32-33). He writes that "the house is the means by which man carves out of the universal space, a special and to some extent private space, and thus separates inner space from an outer space." (p. 33) The outer space is "the space of openness, of danger and abandonment", a place where one must exercise cau-tion. The inner space is "an area protected and hidden, an area in which a person can be relieved of continual anxious alertness, into which he [or she] can withdraw in order to return to him [or her]self." (p. 33) Ideally inner space is the place where one can be oneself. The bound-ary between the inner and outer spaces are the walls of the house. However, the notion of boundary should not be considered as something that limits or confines; instead, the boundary is a point from which growth continues. (Heidegger, 1964, p. 332). In the same manner, the sense of 'home' should broaden as we grow older and venture into the world.

The boundary between the security of the inner space and the insecurity of the outer space is not so abrupt as I have implied:

> . . . When I leave the protection of my house, I do not immediately step into a hostile world. I remain at first in a protective neighbourhood, an area of trusted relationships, of vocation, friendships, etc. Around the individual house in the broader area of that which we call home (Heimat). It thins out slowly from the relatively known through the comparatively unknown, into the completely unknown. (Bollnow, 1961, p. 35)

As I read Bollnow's work I see the possibilities of my own classroom being a home if it provides the atmosphere of the "protective neighbourhood", the opportunity for building "trusted relationships", experiencing "vocation" and developing "friendships". My classroom certainly does not remain the completely unknown, and it can be the intimate and safe haven which develops the security for the child to open.

My attention is drawn to Vandenberg's emphasis on the importance of home in developing "the security which allows the child to open" to the world: "the outside world is explored inside the home" (1975, p. 43). I believe the consequences of creating the security of home in the classroom are similar to those developed in the family home which provides a security for children. The security of home helps to foster "openness toward adults" singularly represented by the teacher (Vandenberg, 1975, p. 44). The teacher can have the same disposition of openness creating a safety for the children to develop confidence and curiosity—an openness to the future. (Vandenberg, 1975, p. 44)

As a teacher I cannot undo the damage that has been committed to a child, but I can create an atmosphere in the classroom where the child can live his or her childhood more fully, which may result in an eagerness to learn.

Getting Back 'Home'

- What are the pedagogical implications of these questions of home in my classroom practice?
- What are the conditions of home in the classroom like?
- Can I create the conditions of home in the classroom?
- Is the experience of being 'at home' in the classroom important for children, and if so, how is it important?
- What is being at home in the classroom like for me as a teacher?
- What is it like to experience 'home' in the classroom?
- Can we do something with this 'homeness'?
- Can it do something to us?

I wanted to understand the answers to these questions, the experiences of being at home through the use of stories from my classroom and those of my childhood memories of home. I was interested in how so many of my colleagues and I take the same education courses at university; we discuss what takes place in our classrooms—the process and the product of that which is created jointly by teacher and students—yet, in actuality, each classroom has a different flavour. Visitors would come and say of my classroom that it was "very relaxed," that the children's discussions resembled "something that took place between trusted friends or family members around the table after dinner," that the atmosphere was "intimate and cozy—much like home." How was that different, I wondered, from so many other classrooms? In what way was my classroom like home?

My understanding of being at home in the world and my memories of home seemed elusive at first. That which I so desperately wanted to reach. and grasp hold of was unseen, in the same way that I could not locate the souvenir from my childhood bedroom during my guided visualization. I wanted to know the essence of the experience of being at home in the classroom.

I began to observe my students more closely and follow the advice of Vivian Gussin Paley (1989) who suggests that to make sense or meaning in the classroom, teachers must spend more time watching children and listening to what they say. (p. 1) My classroom stories began to unfold naturally within the context of everyday events and I found the extraordinary in the ordinary, what Gussin Paley calls the "preoccupation with minutiae." (p. 1) I jotted down notes after morning sharing, often the most vital time of the day, when the children would bring their concerns from home and playground into the classroom. They discussed their own ethical and moral decisions based on their own actions and those of others in their lives. As I grew further attuned to the importance of our discussions, my listening became honed and focused, allowing all of us, teacher and students to delve deeper. Often afterwards, as the children returned to their seats, I would dash down a few words from our discussion on a paper napkin stuffed in my pocket, leftover from morning coffee. The children and I frequently wrote in journals after sharing. This was a time when I could write more from those sharing times: whole dialogues, descriptions of the children's facial expressions, the mood of the room, all part of the meandering path of our discourse. These I would expand at home on the computer or amplify in lengthier writing times in the classroom. As I was thinking about my own past and what I observed in the classroom, I was using those experiences as a text.

I was linking together my present—the classroom and my past—my childhood, as I worked on my own text, for the reflection required in writing about the classroom triggered some of my sweetest memories from home. One such memory was a glimpse of my mother and me tucked into the kitchen nook, a space the size that would permit two people who were comfortable enough with each other to bump hips and elbows without need of an apology. This nook was the place where, while rolling cookie dough, I learned the stories of my family, the truths shared and the truths discovered of the Dohms, the Trudelles, and the Brunelles. Here I learned the significant details that were the essence of their lives: how my grandmother was renowned for her crackshot abilities with the Winchester she packed. It was here that I received 'a snapshot' of how my grandfather courted her and ensured his return the next day by 'forgetting' his pipe on her family gate. All of my memories of home, the pictures and the voices, were not so sweet, however. It would take time for them to surface and take shape, which indeed they did. Over time I came to confront the painful memories and recognize the force they held over me. By writing them down, looking at them and pulling the stratified layers apart, I discovered that they, too, shaped my efforts in making my classroom homey.

I developed my awareness of the meaning of the stories through the narratives themselves. "Among teachers, and also among parents, anecdote is the natural way by which particular concerns of educating and living with children are brought to awareness," writes Max van Manen (1989, p. 232). He continues with:

> Better yet, anecdotal narrative allows the person to reflect in a concrete way on experience and thus appropriate that experience. To anecdote is to reflect, to think. Anecdotes form part of the grammar of everyday theorizing. In a reflective grasping, anecdotes recreate experience but in a transcended (focused, condensed, intensified, oriented, and narrative) form. Thus the act of anecdoting as concrete reflecting prepares the space for hermeneutic phenomenological reflection and understanding. (van Manen, 1989, p. 232)

I wanted to understand the meaning from these stories, to make sense of the classroom situation and to understand what had happened, so that I could explain to myself and others the meaning of my experiences of 'home'. Narrative is the compelling way to make sense of the emotional experience. Narrative helps us to understand how we make meaning of our lives.

My writing grew initially from being a member of a group which consisted of practicing teachers and supervisors of student teachers who were selected by two university professors. It was our intention to discuss stories from our classrooms, find themes within them, and later write those stories. Some of our conversations were taped and transcribed for the purposes of further discussion, analysis and development of the stories into a book. This group provided the impetus for me to write,

as the stories were fresh in my mind after our meetings, and the group discussion and feedback gave a
vitality and resonance to the stories told. I began to
locate the common threads of themes within the stories. The group dissolved over time but I continued to
write and grew ever more keen to probe and expand on
the writing.

"Talking is not sufficient," writes Vivian Gussin
Paley (1989), because in talking we "are interrupted and
distracted" before we can carry any thought too far; we
"censor our failures" and with our colleagues we become
"too self-revealing or too critical of accepted notions and
practices—even of [our] own" and run the risk of having
our audience turn away." (pp. 8-9) She says, "We write
down our thoughts and observations to question and
argue with ourselves; to discover the special significance
of a particular experience." (1989, p. 8) Yet the words
were hard for me to locate, for the ground of the classroom shifts from moment to moment.

The language I used came from the children's conversations—it contains the subtleties embedded in
slang, ellipsis, incomplete sentences, fragments, and
body language. I tried to record my first reactions and
those of the children I watched. I needed to use language that would capture the emotion, mood, and tone
of the experience. The language had to permit me to
tell the story of my experience in my own voice and to
convey my intentions. I knew from reading Michael
Rosen's *Did I hear you write?* (1989) that it is vital to
use what he calls "oral language," i.e., the language
that is said in everyday talk, in our written language,
in order to engage with our own authentic thoughts
and feelings. (pp. 22-23) The thoughts and feelings
that I wanted to engage with were not just my own nor
my parents', but those of my students, their parents,

my colleagues and administrators. What I wanted to create in my work was what Michael Rosen (1989) tells children in his workshops: "Writing is 'like making a photo album" . . . "to preserve things." (p. 24) I wanted to close the door of my classroom at the end of the day, to slam it shut to after school meetings and workshops and write, as Vivian Gussin Paley advocates we teachers do, in order to get the snapshot of the classroom while the action was still there, to capture the words that would trigger the essence of the conversations.

I knew the language I wrote in was authentic, for in my classroom we have a feedback time after sustained writing in which the children read their works, at which time I would read them what I had written about our early morning sharing. Their reaction was one of incredulity at first, then some would become critical and determine the accuracy of the accounts. After one such reading, Aaron, my fifth grade student, said, "Ms. Sinclaire, the way you write it, it's true. It's just that it's almost more than true because you got right to the **important** stuff." Aaron is as eloquent in the simplicity of his statement as Max van Manen (1989) who writes, "And yet writing, true writing, can concretize the experience of the world more pithily, it seems, more to the shaking core (however strange it may seem) than the world as experienced." (p. 240)

The selection for my focus comes from a personal quest. It allows for my intimate attunement to the subject that goes beyond improving the classroom climate to just a homey atmosphere. The language is simple; yet the meaning of the stories is more complex—multi-layered and deep, personal yet universal. Vivian Gussin Paley (1989) reminds me of the need for personal discovery in writing:

But you also need to know your own ideas more intimately; you need to know what makes you different from your colleagues. You have your own inner support of memories, feelings, and instincts. Through these you will find your own questions and follow through in your own ways. (p. 9)

I am bound to my memories, my history, that complex intertwining of past experiences and feelings of which I am composed. They come in to the classroom with me as a part of me each day and they help me to recall, to ask again, "What is the experience of being here like for the child?" I wonder if we can ever escape our 'homes'. Yet, the most positive aspects of my upbringing I recreate in the classroom with my students. For example, I love to read with expression to my students for extended periods of time, just the way I was read to by my father nestled atop his lap. And I value the messing about we do in the classroom with experiments, in the same manner in which I was encouraged to play as a child at the nearby pond and make discoveries with my microscope at home. This is what van Manen (1990) calls "the positive relation of generativity" that enables us through our parenting and teaching to "leave something worthwhile of ourselves behind in our children." (p. 22)

On the other hand, the influence of our homes can have a negative effect of pain, fear and isolation. I recalled those influences and feelings during the guided imagery. What purpose do these memories serve?

In the negative case we reproduce the burden and curse into the lives of our own children. In the positive case we transform our personal problems into something valuable. (van Manen, 1991, p. 22)

In this book I set about in part to understand and attempt to answer that question for myself. I do so in order that I can understand what the experience of home in the classroom is like for children, and also to draw meaning from some of my painful memories of home. At first, I argued with myself about the value of these memories and I said, "That was then. Everything is different now." And the newly awakened person that I am answered, "No. The past is important to who I am today and what I do now. There is a thread from the past that runs through me in all that I do and all that I am."

I am not the child I was, nor do I remain the teenager I was, and yet, in spite of my many passages, life changes and personal identities there is still a "permanent self-sameness" about my nature. (van Manen, 1991, p. 23). The power of the influences of my home and school embedded within my childhood memories leaves its residual effect in how I treat my students. I reflect upon my pedagogical decisions, but I must become aware of the extent to which my pedagogical intents and actions are shaped by my past.

In teaching we are always concerned with the question of preparing children for the future. So the question, "What will I become in the future?" is worth reexamining. My memories of childhood may be thought of as a search backwards in time to discover the present. "The search, however, can be both backwards and forwards. . . . And it can illuminate the present," write Roy Bentley and Syd Butler (1988, p. 11). They state that it is more than "an exercise in reminiscence; it is an active ordering and shaping of events so that one sees not only a beginning, middle and end but also beginnings, middles and ends." (1988, p. 11) Therein lies the hope that my memories which emerge in writing will affect my way of being in the present with children and guide me towards creating a home in the classroom.

Writing provides the attention and focus to sustain, recapture and possibly, for me to understand more. In a letter to a young writer Anais Nin explains her reasons for writing:

> . . . We write to taste life twice, in the moment and in retrospection . . . We write to be able to transcend our life, to reach beyond it . . . We write to teach ourselves to speak with others, to record the journey into the labyrinth, we write to expand our world, when we feel strangled, constricted lonely. . . . (1976, pp. 149-150)

Writing about the events of the classroom and my childhood memories is helping me to speak more intimately, to listen more intensely to my students. It permits me to "make comparisons between the written experience and how I remembered them before I wrote them." I make discoveries "of the experience that lay hidden, half remembered or unthought of." (Rosen, 1989, p. 26) All memories are reconstructions of the past filtered through what has taken place in our lives in the meantime; all childhood experiences are impossible to reclaim as they were experienced in their original condition. For even when we are in the present we are never totally present; therefore, in the past we could never have been totally present. Perhaps the relationship between me and my memories changes over time; certainly in writing about an experience, my relationship and my attitude towards a memory change. In print, I can take charge of the situation; I can replay it, rehearse it, and perhaps even change my response to a real situation in the future.

Writing about looking for home has helped me to evaluate myself, to discern what has been good and what has been bad about the day in the classroom, what has been 'homey' about it. In larger terms, I have evaluated the worth of the good and the bad of my memories of my home. In talking about learning and understanding one's family stories, Elizabeth Stone (1988) writes of the complexity of the influence of our life histories:

> Eventually we come of age and tell the story of our own lives in which the past has become our prologue; we have our own family and invent an ethos for it. This is the stage of transformations, willed or unwilled, the point at which we make our own meanings. Our meanings are almost always inseparable from stories, in all realms of life. And once again family stories, invisible as air, weightless as dreams, are there for us. To make our own meanings out of our myriad stories is to achieve balance—at once a way to be part of and apart from our families, a way of holding on and letting go. (pp. 243-244)

Making meaning from my memories of home is helping me find a place for myself in the classroom and outside of it, a place called home. I have been regenerated through the process; I have honed myself as I am reminded of my calling.

What is my calling? The calling is one of preparing the child in my classroom for being at home in the world. The anecdotes from my own classrooms over a period of three years are the means by which I explore and question how my own classroom helps children to become more at home in the world. First of all, I look at the notion of home at the personal level, to be at home with oneself, i.e., to accept oneself in the context of one's own maturity. Secondly, I delve into home at the meta level—the universal home for the child, a historical, cultural and spiritual home as the child gains maturity. Thirdly, I observe the celebration of the self as both unique and part of a community at home in the world.

That sense of being 'at home' which had been invisible and out of reach at the beginning of my search has become visible to me through my writing. As Max van Manen (1989) observes:

> Writing exercises and makes empirically demonstrable our ability to see. Writing shows that we can now see something and at the same time it shows the limits or boundaries of our sightedness. In writing, the author puts in symbolic form what he or she is capable of seeing. And so practice, in the lifeworld with children, can never be the same again. My writing as a practice prepared me for an insightful praxis in the lifeworld. (I can now see things I could not see before.) Although I may try to close my eyes, to ignore what I have seen, in some way my existence is now mediated by my knowledge. And because we are what we can see (know, feel, understand), seeing is already a form of praxis—seeing the significance in a situation places us in the event, makes us part of the event. Writing, true writing, is authoring, the exercise of authority: the power that authors and gives shape to our personal being. Writing exercises us in the sense that it empowers us with embodied knowledge which now can be brought to play or be realized into action in the performance of the drama of everyday life. (p. 241)

I am changed by the insights I formed from observing and writing about the classroom and my memories. I can never be the person nor the teacher I was before forming these insights about being at home.

2

Being at Home with Each Other

My Home

Ours was a home where my father's authority reigned supreme over all of us, including my mother. There was no room for disobedience and very little room for discussion when viewpoints differed from those of my father's. The story that follows was painful for me to write, for it exposes each one of us in the worst of emotions that arise in a family. Yet, there is value for me in writing this memory and examining it, for in doing so, I wonder how the situation might have been if each of us had acted otherwise. Rereading and discussing the incident allows me the opportunity to reflect on how children experience emotions of fear, anger, powerlessness, and helplessness, and, in considering these ideas, I see how I can be sensitive to those feelings. I can act differently and make the classroom a safe place.

My father's words to us kids were, "You don't have to like me; you **do** have to respect me, even if that means being afraid of me." He says something like that as he puts the razor strap back on the hook behind the bathroom door.

"Where is that kid anyways?" he demands. He spots my brother and drags him, angry, crying, but unrepentant despite his strapping, into the bathroom.

I'm glad Jimmy's getting it. He swore at my mom. I am six and my brother is nine. Sometimes we are bitter enemies but mostly we just avoid each other. My brother doesn't look like he's sorry so he's going to get more.

"No, Fred, no. Oh, no," my mother's voice is shrill. Her vocal chords quake. I cower in the long, dark hall, frightened now. What's he going to do? The door swings open a little. Mom is wringing her hands, her apron. My father grabs my brother's collar and pulls Jimmy down to his knees on the dark linoleum floor by the toilet. My dad jerks the cover and lid of the toilet back with a slamming force. He begins flushing, ramming my brother's head into the raging waters while wrenching his head down by his hair.

"Don't you ever call your mother that again, do you hear me!?" he yells. My dad is crazy with his temper. My brother is gagging, choking for air. He doesn't answer—a sign my father in his fury takes for disobedience. My dad reaches for the soap.

My mother's cries become more shrill as she calls out, "Oh, my God! What am I going to do!?" I come closer, wanting to protect her.

"Stay back, I don't want you here!" she yells at me. The door slams shut again and there is a lot of bumping against the walls inside.

My father shouts menacingly at me, "You heard your mother. You listen to her. . . !" There is a warning within the tone: Or else it could be you.

My mother is screaming! I turn the crystal doorknob and look inside. They don't hear me for all the commotion. Foam gushes from Jimmy's open mouth. He is choking and coughing. He is so red. I am paralyzed by fear. I can't go away, I can't pretend this didn't happen. There is no place to go. I can't help my mother.

She cannot stop this from happening to my brother—perhaps to me too. I'm so scared. I retreat down the hall making myself scarce. A knot tightens inside me, winching in my breath and my heart. I wait. The flushing, screaming, thumping ends and the door slams open. My dad drags my brother by the collar down the hall into the kitchen. Jimmy is scarlet and shaking. I feel sorry for him now.

My father slumps onto the couch to read the newspaper with a sigh, "At last. . . . Now, maybe I can get a little peace in here." He snaps the paper open and retreats behind newsprint. Quietly my brother leaves, quickly, out the back door, softly, out to his friends.

My mother returns to washing the dishes in the nook, more listless than before. Periodically, she wipes her eyes with her apron. I stand close to her and stroke her thin, freckled arm.

"No, no, it's okay. Really," she murmurs, embarrassed to let me see her this way. "No, no, it's okay. There's just something in my eye. Go and play." I press myself closer to her. Our bodies touch, her thigh, my hip. I rub her arm gently, connecting all the freckles on her forearm with my outspread fingers. We are silent. We never talk about it. Maybe it will be me next and I will drown in the water. I can't swim but my brother can.

Silence was our armour. We remained ever-alert, cautious, and timid. Silence shut us off from our reality and temporarily numbed some of the pain we felt. Not talking about it meant my father's eruptive rages didn't exist. Silence and the denial of facts afforded us some safety. But silence kept us from being truly accessible to each other. Silence helped to perpetuate my father's rages. To speak freely would entail trust, and trust was not the case, for we lived in fear of the next outburst. Each time mistrust and fear led us back to silence.

I am puzzled for years by my father's words, "You don't have to like me; you just have to respect me." Is being feared better than being liked? I vow that I will never treat another person this way, never a friend nor an enemy.

Strangely, I muse to a friend, my best days in teaching are those when I am under a pressure that tightens a knot inside me again, that frightens me in ways like the toilet bowl incident. When I trudge back to class after a difficult staff meeting where a colleague is demoralized and silenced, I vow that today my classroom will be a soft, warm, safe cocoon for the children. I listen deeply. I watch with a delicacy. I feel the feelings of each child with the sensitivity of radar. If a child goes beyond the boundaries of acceptability, as my brother did, I wait a little longer to tolerate and give the child room to manoeuvre, even if I can't approve of his actual behavior. I will use language, reason, the sensitive ear and the listening heart to detect the message from the child's demeanour. I encourage my students to treat each other the same way. Being liked won't interfere with respect. I'd rather be liked than feared. And I'm sure that being liked can contribute to respect.

From my brother's toilet bowl punishment I learned many lessons. As a child, regrettably, I learned to hide my feelings and never show my anger. I learned never to get caught, to leave no signs, to plan ahead, to outsmart them, to always be ready.

The lessons I learned have become pivotal in my practice. I have learned that when administrators won't listen to me, I tell them what they want to hear. Then I close the door and do what I believe is right for kids.

From what was a shocking experience I have formed my strong beliefs that how I treat children can be different. As a teacher, I decided that if I touch a child it will be as soft as when a butterfly lights on a shoulder. School is not a place for me to impose my will upon children. It's a place for children to unfold their wings, dry them and fly at their own speed and altitude.

It's funny as I think of it, I don't remember my brother ever calling my mother a name again. I've wondered how he would discipline his children. A little while ago my brother was telling my dad and me about his son stealing money from his mother's purse, at which point my dad suggested a "good paddling" to stop it.

I heard my brother say as he shook his head slowly and hid his eyes from view, "No. Uh, . . . uh. You must never touch a child in anger. Never." I wonder where he learned that.

I wonder what it might have been like if my father had paused and allowed Jimmy to speak. What would it have been like if my father had listened and heard my brother out? There must have been a reason for my brother's disrespect for my mother. What had occurred beforehand? Stopping and listening might have provided an opportunity to discuss the issue and impart something, to teach my brother something. What might my father have learned about my brother and what might I have learned, as a consequence, about speaking up and being listened to?

Creating Home for a Child

I like to think about what I have learned from this experience that I can take into the classroom to make it 'homey'. 'Homey', in the sense of being comfortable with each other, to know each other and be at ease with one another. The heart of any relationship for me is to be listened to and heard beyond the words alone.

Being heard creates a home for John, a big, red-faced boy who uses his size to frighten others into sub-

mitting to his desires, in the next story. I listen carefully
to hear him tell his story and I get to know him better.
Listening to John's story allows me to see him in the
context of his world; being heard allows him to be
accepted. He tells me his family's history while I am
silent and patient in listening. I stay with what he is
revealing so that we can achieve a certain intimacy. In
listening, I hear his pain and uprootedness and, as a
result, I see him differently. John, too, is changed in the
telling and in being heard.

It is an early fall afternoon and my student teacher
has assigned a project: an environmental art collage.

"If it's okay with you, Elaine, I'll just stay in the
room and work on one, too."

"Oh, sure," she answers, looking a little curious,
but blinded by the whir of children moving about her
excitedly. Some are gathering scissors and glue, some
are fetching friends so they can sit close and be together.
For it is in the act of being together with someone they
trust that they can fully 'be', to be themselves.

This is an opportunity for me to sit and get to know
some of the new students and get reacquainted with others, some of the quiet ones who did not show much of
themselves last year in my class.

I choose to sit at the long table between Nadine, a
quiet fourth grade student and John, a fifth grader with
a report card that indicates this will be a difficult year for
all of us. He has already shoved and punched those students who have not let him be "first." He is reluctant to
sit with the others on the carpet and sits off a few feet,
with a space around him, an invisible moat that seems
dangerous for him and for the rest of us to cross.

Nadine darts looks at me whenever John leaves the
table for something he has forgotten. One looks says, "I
hate him. He's always. . . . " Any number of confronta-

tional behaviors could fit: pounding, poking, grabbing, kicking, shrieking, even farting.

He returns and bumps into the table. Nadine's design is in shambles. Cut-out toucans, orioles and finches shower over the table and onto the floor. "Stop that!" she shrieks. "You're always doing that." She directs her attention to me, and pleads angrily, "Can't I sit somewhere else? I hate him. He's so clumsy . . . and mean. He does it on purpose!"

I look at her and sympathize. He is a brute much of the time. But this time he didn't do it intentionally.

Teachers often say of a big boy, "He doesn't **know** his size." He does not have a self-awareness.

Later in the year, John will cry out in a tantrum, "I'm fat and everyone makes fun of me. That's why I can hit them." Any remark, any look can be misconstrued by John as a slight about his body, his person and, therefore, a right to retaliate with abuse. He **is** sorry and embarrassed to have to apologize but if I weren't there he'd probably be jeering at her misfortune.

I say to Nadine, "I'll think about another place. Do you have some ideas?" She's still angry and wants immediate action. She sulks, head down. Words alone cannot restore her dignity.

I want to talk to Nadine about her design—dazzling colors against a midnight background, an array much like her own fiery temperament and dark, concealing looks. But John wants the attention; he's giddy with the need for it. When I turn my attention to him he settles down into a seat and becomes calm. He begins by telling me of his moves: Richmond, Kerrisdale, Oliver, Tunkwa.

"We just keep moving. Just when I get used to one school and one teacher, we move again," his voice contains genuine regret. He makes each stop sound as though he were reaching Nirvana before being wrenched away to a new location all over again.

"Seven schools since Kindergarten! I've never had a whole year at one school yet. Probably not grade five this year either."

Is there to be a reprieve for me and the students? At the same time my thoughts about him soften.

"It's 'cause my dad, his last boss, well, they didn't get along. My dad did all this work for him, see? And when the customers came in and saw how much the plumbing shop had changed, my dad's boss said, yeah, that he'd been working hard. He never said it had been my dad's idea and that my dad done it. Nothing!" He pauses and says with justification, "So, my dad quit and that's when we left Richmond."

"Tunkwa, do you know Tunkwa?" he asks.

"No, I've never heard of it."

"Well, that's where my dad comes from. It's really nice up there." His voice grows more excited, almost cheerful. "We go up and stay in a cabin. We stay there instead of my Grandpa's house because when my Grandpa died he never left anything to my dad. Nothing, not even his watch!" Even Nadine looks up at this and holds her scissors poised.

"My dad's brothers got it all. And what they left behind, the neighbours took," he laments. I am wondering if John's excessive demands in class are because he thinks his own brother receives more attention than he does at home. Does his father's story repeat itself again? Later, in discussion with his parents, I learn of the fighting between John and his brother. John's mother says of her son's behavior, "Oh, I don't know why John's like that. He's **always** been like that. He's better now, you shoulda' seen him in Kindergarten!! We treat them both equally. Of course, John's no athlete and no scholar," she adds, shaking her head and rolling her eyes. The brother is. His father openly admits to preferring the other boy, despite the boy being his stepson. "My Grandpa and my dad never got along . . . they always fought. Ever since my dad was a teenager. He ran him off the place with a shotgun and my dad didn't even have a cent when he left!" John says this with a tone of righteousness and indignation, as though he were his father feeling the pain again and repeating the story himself.

"I never got to meet my grandpa . . ." John's voice becomes wistful as he traces the losses of continuity in his life back farther in time.

This story keeps repeating itself with its themes of rejection, abandonment and loss, being a black sheep, disapproval and lack of recognition. Is what John's grandfather did to his own son being repeated? Is John's father now doing it to **his** own son? Is John carrying on the cycle with other children? We keep repeating the stories of our families, making them our stories and our own ways of being in the world. Can understanding the meaning of the story stop the cycle?

"But we go up there anyway," he says, his face brightening. "And someday," he takes a big breath after emphasizing "someday" and finishes by repeating, ". . . someday my dad's gonna buy my Grandpa's place back from the guy who's got it now." His voice contains the confidence that only a child can hold about the future. It's an assurance that everything will come to pass exactly the way it would in the dream, not a detail changed with no unexpected hardships: And they lived happily ever after.

John enjoys telling me about himself and his family. He wants me to know him. I am listening to know him at a deeper level. Robert Coles (1989) speaks of a lecture on psychiatric patients that would resonate through his career. The professor told him, "The people who come to see us bring us their stories. They hope they tell them well enough so that we understand the truth of their lives. They hope we know how to interpret their stories correctly. We have to remember that what we hear is **their story**." (p. 7) At no time in my university education had I been told to listen to students' stories. I'd been taught to teach abstractions in concrete ways, to listen and attend, to check my wait time, to play back tapes of my teaching and analyze them. I am teaching myself to listen to students' stories to understand how they make meaning of their lives. In John's case, it is as Carl Rogers expresses, that those meanings are yet inaudible to the person who is speaking. (1969, p. 227) Rogers says that "listening can enable the other to hear herself, hear the sound . . . of her ownmost needs and desires." (p. 227) He describes the deep satisfaction he feels when, as he puts it, "I can really hear someone." (Rogers, 1969, p. 227) He writes:

> I believe I know why it is so satisfying to me to hear someone. When I can really hear someone, it puts me in touch with him. It enriches my life. . . . There is also another peculiar satisfaction in it. When I really hear someone, it is like listening to the music of the spheres, because, beyond the immediate message of the person, no matter what that might be, there is the universal, the general. Hidden in all the personal communications which I really hear there seem to be orderly psychological laws, aspects of the awesome order which we find in the universe as a whole. So there is both the satisfaction of hearing this particular person and also the satisfaction of feeling oneself in some sort of touch with what is universally true. (Rogers, 1969, p. 227)

I am listening to John's need to be settled in one place, to find a home for himself and his family. And I am also listening to his father's search for that home he feels he lost unjustly to his brothers. I am recognizing their needs to be at home wherever that home might be geographically located. Of course, these are not John's words per se, but below his words alone he may have the desire to be taken into the fold of his family with equal acceptance and appreciation as that received by his stepbrother. He needs to find his true place there. Carl Rogers asks himself what it is like to listen at the level that involves such interpretation:

> So I have learned to ask myself, can I hear the sounds and sense, the shape, of this other person's inner world? Can I resonate to what he is saying, can I let it echo back and forth in me, so deeply that I sense the meanings he is afraid of yet would like to communicate, as well as those meanings he knows? (1969, p. 227)

I excuse myself from the students to give Elaine an idea of how long children need to clean up in September. When she rings the bell, John is disappointed that his time with me is up.

"I really enjoyed talking to you," he says. This is an unusually mature and polite response from a ten year old.

"I enjoyed hearing your story and getting to know you, John."

Something has changed between us. I had read his records with the list of schools attended and I knew what effect that has on children. But to hear that list translated into a personal narrative by John—to hear his story told by him—is truer than facts alone. That I know those things about him, and he knows that I know, changes our relationship. He knows that I listen and that I care, for I have given neither advice nor solutions. I accept him. I am willing to share his burden with him. He is not alone. I will be there for him.

He seeks me out nightly to say goodbye as though I were a friend. And for a few days, just a few, he doesn't get in any scraps with the other kids and he doesn't insult anyone. From this time on he sits on the carpet with the others. He is amongst us now.

Rogers describes what happens when he truly hears a person and his or her meanings, and when he lets the person know that he has heard the meanings:

> There is first of all a grateful look. He feels released. He wants to tell me more about his world. He surges forth in a new sense of freedom. I think he becomes more open to the process of change.

> I have often noticed . . . that the more deeply I can hear the meanings of this person, the more there is that happens. One thing I have come to look upon as almost universal is that when a person realizes he has been deeply heard . . . in some real sense he is weeping for joy. It is as though he were saying, 'Thank God, somebody has heard me. Someone knows what it's like to be me.' In such moments I have had the fantasy of a prisoner in a dungeon, tapping out day after day a Morse code message, 'Does anybody hear me? Is there anybody there? Can anyone hear me?' And finally, one day, he hears some faint tappings which spell out 'Yes'. By that one simple response he is released from his loneliness; he has become a human being again. (1969, p. 227)

I wonder how many of my students are living in their "private dungeons" who give no sign of it from the outside. I have to listen very hard to hear the faint messages from within. In listening to John, I accept him as he is and help him to listen to himself, and to become the human being he most deeply wants to be. Can I do this each day with the amount of distractions in the classroom? I agonize over so few opportunities to actually sit with children for extended periods of time to listen to their stories.

Once a trusting relationship has been established, children seek their teacher out for one-to-one time after school. In the next story, the child wants to ask advice and discuss something of the most intimate nature, a subject for which I have no teacher preparation. What serves to guide me in our talk together are my intentions for her and calling upon my own experiences in life.

Home is Finding Our Self

"Can we help?" It's a common after-school plea from students, especially those who would like a closer connection to the teacher. Of course, some want the adventure of climbing ladders armed with staple removers and the ecstasy of ripping paper off the classroom walls in would-be wanton acts of destruction.

But today it's Deanna and Bethany, two fifth graders who want to help while getting help in the form of advice. Usually it's a matter of older boys, flirting, necking, petting, getting married, not getting married, living alone, or being an 'old maid'—all affairs of the heart and loins.

"Well. . . ." I hesitate when they ask to help because finding work for children is often more work for me. But

I sense a tension in the girls that needs to be expressed through busy work together. They sort papers halfheartedly but keep circling my desk.

"Okay, it's done," Deanna says sadly and comes up very close to me. She is almost on my lap, she is so close, holding on to the back of my chair and touching my shoulder. I look at her face with its expression both tense and forlorn. Deanna was sexually abused by her father. She disclosed her story last year in a program intended to safeguard children against such crimes. Her memories were hazy at first, allowing room for doubt. Later, each image became clearer. Her mother had to listen and believe. Deanna's grades fell from poor to worse and she became obsessed talking about it, constantly rerouting every discussion back to "what my dad did to me." Deanna uses her charm and her coyness to manipulate her many boyfriends. It works for a while until they find someone prettier. Deanna's face looks old, as though she knew too much too early and it drained off her youth.

"Ms. Sinclaire," she begins with a wheedling tone. I respond with a nod.

"When you were a kid, did you dress up for Halloween?"

"Sure. Of course."

"Like what? What did you dress up as? What **were** you?"

"Oh, different things. A gypsy girl a lot. I liked that. Lots of beads and skirts, a scarf wrapped around my hair. Rouge. Lipstick. That was me. There were others, too."

"Like what?"

"Flowers, some kind of flower in Grade one. My mother made the costume out of crepe paper. I can't remember much. Then there were others. A tramp, you know, a hobo the last time. But my favourite was always the gypsy girl."

I study Deanna's expression. Her face winces even more as she forms a question to venture with me. I put my arm around her softly as a reassurance.

Deanna giggles a little and puts her hand up to her mouth. Her head turns a little to one side and she bounces it back and forth between her shoulders to build up a silliness that will conceal her intention. "I was thinking. . . . " Her eyes roll upwards.

"Yes?" I ask softly.

Then she snuggles beside my shoulder, hiding her eyes from my sight and blurts out, "I was thinking of dressing up for Halloween as a hooker." She deliberately steps away from me to gauge my reaction.

I reel a bit and take my time. I am no prude. How can I reach out to her to show her the way? What words can I say? I am a woman who has had experiences with men that have sometimes left me feeling shamed and diminished as, I suppose, Deanna feels. I suspect she measures the extent of love she can receive by what she can offer sexually. What can I say? For as a teacher, I represent morality; I have an image to uphold in the community. It is too dangerous to share a personal story from my life with Deanna; I cannot risk talk. I feel somewhat complicit in the crimes against this little girl for not speaking up and letting her know that I have been hurt too.

I recall two dances: the same location, two different dates in the fall on campus at the university twenty years before. I went to them both.

To the first, I wore a simple mini-length button up-the-front black dress with a white collar. My accessories were pristine: white stockings and black shoes. My long, dark curly hair was tamed by combs that held back all but my long bangs—an image straight from the pages of *Seventeen* magazine. I danced all night and the boys were well-mannered. They responded to my image and I, in turn, responded to their treatment of me. I was demure. They fawned over me and I was ladylike.

I was misinformed that the second dance was a costume party. I dressed for the occasion in a cave woman outfit which I had excitedly finished sewing that same evening. It was a leopard skin print with one shoulder! I wore sandals that laced up my legs. My hair was wild and loose, suggesting that I was, too. Groups of boys stood around and talked about me in ways that left me embarrassed. I was the sole young woman in costume, but did they **believe** I was wearing a disguise? A few boys danced with me but they were rough and pressed their bodies against my costume. I felt stupid and cheap. I had rapidly forgotten that my costume was a case of mistaken identity. I **was** the costume to them. In my **own** mind I had **become** something of the costume because of their response to the image. How quickly it all happens.

Waiting for an Answer

Deanna's been waiting for my response. "Well, **would** you? Would **you** dress like that? A hooker?" Her fists are tight.

"No. Because. . . ."

She interrupts. "Why **not**? **Tell** me." Her voice is insistent.

"Because when you dress a certain way, **even** if it's innocent, people identify you with your costume. They think you **are** your costume!" My voice is intense. This is too important to hang back. This is a lesson in life that must be said and she must hear it.

"So you wouldn't do it?"

"No, I **wouldn't** do it." My voice softens as I say, "We women have to be **careful** . . . **all** the time. We have to be careful of the image we give off. People can make mistakes about us. Afterwards, there isn't anything we can do to change the impression. And then **we** start to believe we **are** the costume, that we **are** the way people see us."

Deanna's nodding now.

I take her tiny shoulders in my hands and think, "this is a little eleven-year old girl trying to sort out so much by herself." "And **you**, Deanna. This is **important** for you. Because after your experience with your dad I don't want you to think of yourself that way. Your dad made a mistake with you. But it's not **your** fault. And I don't want anyone thinking of you as a hooker. **Especially** you. You're **not** that."

"It's just a costume," she giggles defensively.

"It's **not**. It's more."

"Yeah. I guess so."

Deanna is so light and tiny. I encircle her with my arms and hug her but she cannot trust enough to rest her weight against me. Deanna is sad; Bethany joins her. There are no easy answers, and Deanna must solve this on her own. What to wear? **Who to be?**

"Gotta go. Gotta think up a costume. I don't know! Well, see ya." There is frustration and disappointment in the quest.

Every day it's the same thing. Deanna reports in, "I don't know who to be. Maybe I won't wear a costume. Maybe just a mask. But I **want** to be something **good**."

Deanna wants an identity. Something that can show off her true self, to **"be"** her. Something that is larger and truer and bigger—something to become. I can't help. She must find it on her own.

Deanna must struggle to find the right costume, her true identity, and I must watch over her while she does so, standing back enough to leave her room to discover herself so that she might begin again to grow.

"It's almost Halloween. And I **still** don't have anything." Deanna is shaking her head at me as though my words of counsel are to blame.

It's the morning of the Halloween party. As the mist rises over the back field, crowds of kids throng the back door of the classroom, our private entry way. They hammer on the back door to be let in so they can pile their brownies, pop, rice krispie squares, and cookies on the back counter. Their arms are weighted down by bags of costumes hidden until this afternoon when we will be transformed.

"Where's Deanna? Where's Bethany?" I ask the class while doing attendance.

"Late."

"Late, but they're coming."

The back door swings open and in they come. Deanna is grinning. Her cheeks are Macintosh red and her eyes twinkle. She is carrying a huge stuffed pillowcase.

"I've got my costume! I made it last night. I'm gonna be a chicken. Beth and me sewed the feathers on till eleven—that's why we're late."

"Oh, not **real** feathers, Ms. Sinclaire. Don't worry!" Bethany assures me.

"And I've been practicing chicken sounds!" Deanna giggles and clucks a little for us.

Several days later, the secretary comes down the hall to my classroom and says, "It's the phone for you. It's Deanna's mom on the line." I follow her down to the office.

"Ms. Sinclaire? It's Mrs. Carver—Deanna's mom. I thought this would be a good time to catch you." She hesitates and we make small talk until she returns to the purpose of her call.

"I just wanted to say thank you for what you said to Deanna. About the **costume**."

"Oh, yes. I **had** to say something."

"Well, I don't know **what** you said. But she didn't wear it. Not for Halloween night either. She just came home and put it away. She was very determined."

"Thank you for letting me know.

"Thank you."

Deanna's helplessness as a child, and as an abused child, makes an appeal to me. My presence in her life may be some guarantee of security. She can call on me for help; yet, if I fail to respond and give her the security she needs I will leave her isolated with only her own resources. Her choices depend on our common experience together, that of child and adult, who, in this case, is the teacher.

What matters when we first meet a child in need is our intention. (Langeveld, 1975, p. 7). The personal help I lend to Deanna is through a life experience that could not have been anticipated. There is no preparation in my teaching or in any teacher-proof violence-prevention package to deal with Deanna's quandary about a costume or an identity.

Deanna wants the security to be something "good"; she has aspirations to transcend the event which has marred her view of herself. She wants the reliability of someone she can trust to inform and advise her in her life. You could demand, "Where is the mother in all this?" But Deanna's mother may be dealing with her own feelings about what happened between her husband and daughter and her own responsibility in the matter. However, she is not present at this moment to help her daughter. In this case, it is the teacher in whom the child trusts, the one with whom she has continuity for the school year. Ideally, that continuity would last long

enough until Deanna reaches maturity and can understand what has taken place and develop her own healthy
sense of self. (Langeveld, 1975, pp. 9-10)

Deanna will need help to integrate her past, her present and her future, not by concealing, disguising or
suppressing facts but by giving them their place. The
past must be seen as true, yet kept in its place. "Good
things, even the best things in life, come to an end . . . ,
unless you make them part of your own future, of the
best qualities of your future," writes Langeveld. (1975,
p. 11) So it is with bad things—Deanna could make them
part of her future or receive personal help to find new
ways of being that can free her from the event.

I realize that the past has become an orientation
towards the future: the devastation of sexual abuse
becomes a livable aspect of the present. Deanna must
learn how to conduct herself—**how** to be—as well as
who to be. As adult and child, together we must see
the possibilities for her to have a better life. So it is with
the child whose parents have recently divorced, as well
as the child whose sibling has died of cancer. We must
help each child to gain a new perspective: "Yes, at one
time you all lived together and mommy and daddy loved
each other and you. But then they couldn't settle their
differences. They decided to live apart. Now, each of
them still continues to love you. You are a child who is
loved by two parents." In the same way, Deanna must
not think of herself as the symbol of what might have
been her costume—that of a prostitute. We must help
children to see themselves positively. The only acceptable way for Deanna to act in the face of the irrational
crime committed against her is to act in a manner that
would help her to present herself the way she would
want others to see her, and in the way she would like to
see herself. In this particular case, to act accordingly

would be to dress in a way that represents her, to be something "good" in ways that help her create her own identity.

How do I help this child? How can she continue to help herself in my absence? I have to consider my intentions for Deanna and be sincere with her in order to help her repair the way she sees her self and presents her self to others.

I may fail with Deanna. She may fail. But it's worth a try.

For two years after I leave that school, Bethany and Deanna remain in contact with me by phone. It is always Bethany who calls, usually with Deanna in the background. Deanna speaks to me with nervousness in her voice for the first few minutes, and only after Bethany has exhausted all her own news. Bethany calls me by herself at the end of her seventh grade to tell me of her year-end certificate with its merit badges. "Do you remember the ones? With Sunnyview Elementary on them and the little round stickies? Well, I got seven of them, one for Writing, and one for Athletics, and . . . oh," she whines, "I can't remember what else. But there's seven of them. Yeah. And you know what else? You'll never guess!"

"What?"

"I got the certificate for Most Improved Student." I tell her how proud I am of her and keep to myself the notion that I might have had some hand in shaping part of her success.

We linger on the subject of her achievement and she rambles on enthusiastically about how high school will be until there is a lull.

"How is Deanna doing?" I ask.

The excitement evaporates from the conversation and Bethany answers with sadness and disdain in her voice. "Oh, okay, I guess. I mean . . . we're still friends but we don't see much of each other. She hangs around with a completely different crowd now." Bethany's wording is careful as she reveals, "They smoke and drink and do other stuff. I don't know. She's just different." Her tone is one of shame for and loss of the former friendship. Bethany casually adds, "Deanna, she wants to have a baby now."

I share Bethany's feelings of emptiness and loss. I am overcome by a sense of responsibility, for I left the school at the end of our year together. If I had just stayed there for two more years, then, she might have had someone to come and talk to after school. If I could just make Deanna understand, if I could just make her love and accept herself again, I could make her alive and whole again.

What had been an intimate exchange in the classroom between Deanna and me came from an atmosphere of trust and my attunement to her. But there is a closer connection to her that tugs at me. There is a meaning for me in her story, and even deeper memories surface from my own past that bring me closer to her experience and feelings.

Memories of Childhood

As I write the anecdotes from the classroom, I revisit my own feelings of helplessness as a child, where, like Deanna, I was unable to identify fully those feelings, nor was I able to claim my own rights. Within my self-reproach for leaving Deanna and my longing to restore her, lies a connection to a memory from my own childhood that is evoked gradually from my feelings about her. At first, my memory is but a mood, then slowly images take shape from the mood, enough to be a memory that forms a story awakened from my childhood. The story is about a deer my father shot, a deer that I so loved that I wished to bring it back to life again.

ॐ

"It's your father and it looks like he's got something on top of the car. Oh, I'm just glad he made it home safely and in one piece," my mother sighs as the lines return between her eyebrows after a week of my dad being away on a hunting trip. We both peer through the glass on the back porch door without stepping out into the November night air. "Put on your sweater and we'd better go out to say hello," she says and remembers, "and don't forget your shoes." She knows I always tiptoe out without them, even in January.

My father is talking excitedly and he waves to the top of the Ford where I see small hooves dangling over the roof.

"Spotted him across the river at St. Anne's Creek. Shot him right there on the river bank. Geez, the water was cold! He stuck his head out of a dense bush when I was squatting with my trousers down. I just reached for my .308 and shot him. Straight up in the air he jumped, then sideways. He must've run a hundred feet, then I didn't see him anymore. I'm crossing the river in my long johns because I don't want to get my melton cloth pants wet. Afterwards I hung my long johns up in a tree, and you know, I left 'em there. Darn it! The water was half way up my hips. And there it was—the deer laying there dead on the other side of the river." He just keeps talking, reliving the hunt and I keep looking at the shiny little hooves tethered to the car top carrier, each one about the size of my wrist.

"I had these two sticks to balance me with the deer laying around my neck. Of course I had the front legs tied together . . . but if that current had got me, it would've dragged me under. . . ."

"Oh, Fred," my mother says, sounding worried.

"Yeah. Dressed it out right there by the river bank and carried it up to the truck. Left the innards in a heap with the ravens gathering. An hour later I came back and there was nothing left," he reports. I am stunned. I wonder why he would go back.

He hauls the deer from the truck, unlashing the ties and slings a rope about its neck and hindquarters. "It's clean and it'll keep till morning. I'll skin and butcher it then. I'm too weary now. Boy, that was a long drive," he says, hoisting the carcass to dangle head down from the rafters of the garage. "It'll be safe here. Well, let's go in get something to eat, eh?" he says. "Boy, I sure need to clean up. I don't smell too fresh."

"Carollyne, turn off the lights there and make sure the door's closed tight," my mother says and we follow the porch light into the warmth of the kitchen. I sit at the table and he talks and she mostly listens. But I don't know what they're saying. The words don't mean anything to me. I can only think of the little buck hanging upside down in our garage. Its antlers are formed into fuzzy black nubs. Its eyes are ringed by soft tilted shadows and dense lashes. Its face, so sweet. I am saddened by its beauty and dulled by its loss of life.

"She's tired, Fred, leave her alone," I hear my mother say as my father nudges my arm. My whole body, listless, rocks back and forth. I am powerless to move. "It's time to go to bed," I hear their voices in chorus.

In my room I don't sleep and I don't cry. I just sit on the edge of my bed fondling the chenille balls of the bedspread in my fingers. My father talks on and on and I hear the news on the t.v. The shower runs for a while. And then there is quiet.

I stand on my bed and look outside into the night. The sky is all blue velvet lit up with rhinestones like an evening dress. "If only," I think, "If only I could bring it to life and make it free again." I keep looking into the night as if looking harder at one spot for a long time will make me able to see into the depths of it and beyond. I step softly down the wooden staircase, past my brother's room on the landing, careful not to trip on his skates, down through the long hallway past my parent's room where I hear their steady breathing. I get the flashlight from the drawer in the kitchen and I tiptoe to the porch door where I lift the button, muffling its click and holding the latch to one side. I let myself out, all the while holding my breath. In my bare feet I step down the cement pathway where frost is already forming, leaving traces of my toe prints.

"This door always squeaks," I think, remembering that no one will be listening to the opening of a garage door at this time of the night. I leave it ajar, with the stars alone to light us. I look at the beautiful face of the deer in the moonlight. His eyes still glisten and I run my fingertips delicately over his lids, tracing lightly the lines that frame his eyes. I touch his eyelashes with the back of my hand. So thick and stubbly. My aunt used to give me butterfly kisses with her lashes flicking against my cheeks. I step closer, my breath leaving its mark in the night air and gently press my cheek against his, hoping to transfer all the warmth and life of my body into his. Hot tears roll down my cheeks and fall on his fur. I wrap my arms around his neck and hold him tightly, as though he were some huge teddy bear, that, through some unfortunate turn of fate, I must console. I would give everything I own, everything I love, even my own life, to have him be alive and free now. Everything to give back his innards and his pride and be away from here now.

As I touch his fur, I am surprised he is not soft, but rough. "Perhaps the robber girl's reindeer in The Snow Queen felt this way," I think. "If only I can just love him enough tonight," I think, "maybe tomorrow when everybody wakes up, he will be gone."

I sleep late the next morning and linger a long time over breakfast. "No, I don't feel like shreddies. No, not oatmeal either. No, I don't want any toast."

"Well, what do you want then?" my mother is getting annoyed with me.

"Nothing. I don't want anything," I say, staring out the kitchen window at the garage.

When I go out there to look, there are just big hunks of meat.

Connections to Childhood Create a Home in the Classroom for Children

In these memories I rediscover my feelings of helplessness as a child. I could not stop my father from hunting and killing animals nor could I have changed his insensitivity towards me. It was impossible for me to have brought the deer back to life. I was as much tethered by the unspoken rules of silence in my family as the deer was tethered to the roof. My anger and hurt at the killing of the beautiful deer remained unexpressed, for to voice them would have meant ridicule or punishment.

I discover something of myself in this spiralling back into the memories of the past brought to the surface by writing. I locate sources of my empathy with those who feel powerless. Deanna is helpless over what has happened to her; she cannot change the fact that her father molested her many times as a toddler and as a young girl. She is powerless to speak of her anger for she hasn't yet identified it. She is unable to find the help she seeks from her mother.

I visit my own innocence and forgive myself for the burden of guilt I have carried around as I unveil the forces that have moulded me. In my memory of myself as a teenager, I, too, wanted to be "something good" and wondered what that search might bring. After the dance I yearned to cast off the feeling of being soiled; I wanted a second chance to be made new again.

Now, in visiting these memories, I gain control of and reshape my life. I recognize, too, that I am not alone, nor is Deanna; there are many experiences common to all of us, as I begin to share these stories with my close friends. I bring myself closer to my students as I believe that there are second chances, in fact, many chances, for us to 'breathe life' into ourselves if we discover and claim them. I am saddened by the news of Deanna that Bethany has passed on to me, and yet, I have hope that she will have other chances, too.

As a teacher, I identify with the image of the child who longs to bring the deer to life as I wish I could restore Deanna. It is a futile act for I cannot erase what has happened to her. I cannot be Deanna's parent to spend my time exclusively with her. All I could hope to do is to help her understand what has happened and impart what I can from my own experience. Yet, I am tethered again by the moral constraints of my profession not to reveal too much about myself for fear that my words may put me in jeopardy with the community where I teach. For a little while, at least, the influence of our discussion together had an effect on the choices Deanna made. Deanna needs a continuous 'home' for discussion with someone who can listen and risk enough to share something of her own experience that she can use. My memories of the powerlessness of childhood placed me closer to the feelings of the child in order to help her with a decision, if only for a while.

The quest for meaning in childhood memories should bring teachers closer to our students as we revisit those feelings which remind us of how it is to be a child. There are lessons for me to learn in revisiting these memories: lessons about what it means to be sensitive to children, lessons about listening to what children say and don't say, in other words, about being attentive to their needs. Examining how it was in the past reveals to me the origins of my beliefs and practice in being with children.

As teachers, we must not over-romanticize childhood; instead, we must remember the powerlessness of children, the cruelties they suffer, as well as their joy. We can be more aware of the present in our students if we connect with our own past, not merely specific facts or conclusive evidence, but a connection with an overall truth that runs through our lives.

To remember our childhood deeply is to plumb the depths of our experience and dredge for meanings. Only by revisiting the past did I understand the casing of rules that constricted my childhood, the silence that permeated our house and the sadness I felt then, but was unable to articulate until now.

John, Deanna and Bethany have tugged at my heartstrings, the cords of which are directly tied to my own memories of home. In being with my students and listening to their stories and problems, I do more than merely recollect the events from my home; I remember how it was—the very mood of it. The texture of the concrete things from home awaken the longings I still hold from childhood. As an adult today, I cannot undo what has taken place in my own childhood, but as a teacher who is side by side with children every day, I can use my memories of childhood to respond more closely to their needs. My memories keep me in touch with the experiences of my students. The memories of childhood are a part of what makes me consider the possibilities of how we can make the classroom home for us.

3

The Classroom— A Home for Exploration

The Atmosphere of Home

In this chapter, I describe the atmosphere of the class- room. I begin with a story and conclude with sharing how we should be with one another, children and teacher.

At the end of the day I have some time to myself to think in peace and reflect on particular moments in the day. I think about how the children decided on a 'fair' rotating seating plan for our new couch and chair, how they freed the bird that flew into our classroom, and how they dealt with a name-calling incident during morning sharing. I ask myself, "Are these moments made special because I choose them or are they special in their own right?" Perhaps the atmosphere of "these special moments" is a condition that we perceive, rather than a condition which exists outside ourselves (Vandenberg, 1975, p. 37).

The moments I consider are very ordinary; it is the exchange between us, students and teacher, that makes them extraordinary. The extraordinary quality has every- thing to do with an atmosphere of the classroom that creates a sense of well being for all, teacher and students. (van Manen, 1986, p. 33)

The atmosphere created contributes to the classroom being a special place where we give children opportunities "to explore the outside world" without having to be in it. (van Manen, 1986, p. 33). To some extent, school is a cocoon, a place of safety, preventing children from access to some of the realities of life for which they are not yet prepared. To a greater extent, school is a place where the teacher expands the "private and personal space of home" . . . "to take in larger "public or community space." The classroom becomes a place of exploration when the school forms a bridge between "home and the larger world." (van Manen, 1986, p. 33)

Atmosphere is created in the physical space of the classroom in the activities we engage in and how we experience them. But more importantly, atmosphere is created in the way that the "teacher is present to the children, and the way children are present to themselves and to the teacher." (van Manen, 1986, p. 36)

Let me illustrate with an anecdote from my own classroom which demonstrates how the atmosphere of the classroom serves to create a place for exploration into the world.

One morning, during sharing, Judd has his territory on the carpet invaded. He retaliates by uttering a string of angry curses at Roey. I turn and ask Judd to repeat what he has just yelled. He mumbles the words out.

"A little louder, I can't quite hear," I say.

Judd can tell from the tone of my voice, that I am not threatening him. He repeats the words. "You said that?" I ask, looking incredulous.

"Yeah," he laughs, his cheeks flushing.

"Judd calls me that all the time," Roey rejoinders, his head on one side.

"And that's not all," Allan adds, his eyes bugging out. "Judd's got more. He always says. . . ."

I start laughing, and so do the other students. We are laughing at the absurdity of the words.

A few minutes later we are all sharing inane, insulting remarks and chuckling together. Finally, there is a lull in the insults and a few quiet moments for reflection. "They really don't mean very much, do they, Ms. Sinclaire? I mean, they're just names, aren't they?" Andrea says.

"Yeah, and they are quite funny," Elizabeth adds.

"Sometimes they hurt, but now they just seem silly," Rollie joins in. We sit quietly, happy and still, enjoying each other's company and our thoughts. The taboo topic of curses has been openly dealt with in the classroom. We are learning a lesson—we can think and use language to discuss the problems before us.

The silence created by our discussion takes over the room. We pause, and our thoughts and feelings hush the room, taking up the absence of sound. The silence has an atmosphere that is different from the busy quiet during a math quiz. We are steeped in our own experiences and memories as our thoughts resonate within us in the contemplative mood of the room.

The silence after our classroom eruption and the subsequent discussion lingers with me after school in my private reverie. I hope the atmosphere of that silence lingers long enough for my students to know that conflict can be resolved through discussion; that confrontation can be avoided; and that humor and understanding can result. I might have handled the problem a different way, by deliberately ignoring, by pretending not to hear, or by shushing their comments, but I didn't. Instead, I listened to the voices more intently to detect more than the insults alone. Those voices are hard to hear and the meanings difficult to discern for all the traffic in the classroom, but to not pay heed to them is dangerous. The way I am present for the children in the classroom creates an atmosphere of safety for the children to explore their disputes and struggles for power.

What does this atmosphere consist of Vandenberg (1975) refers to the elements of pedagogic atmosphere as "life-feelings" which he describes as emotions that underlie feelings, and moods that underlie emotions, and, finally, states of mind that underlie all three. When taken together—emotions, feelings, and moods—these "life-feelings" or dispositions shape our stance towards the future and to life in general and with others. (p. 39) What dispositions contribute to a student's learning and exploring his or her world? What dispositions must the teacher possess to teach and to create the conditions for students' risk-taking and exploration? How do the dispositions of teacher and students become attuned with each other to form then atmosphere? (Vandenberg, 1975, pp. 39-40)

In the next story I consider the dispositions that go to make up atmosphere, as I observe my students, and in particular, Cristina, a child who is said to be "difficult and stubborn" by her former teachers. I want to see her through my own eyes in the first week of school. I need to remain open and attuned to her in order for us to develop a relationship that will help her learn and find friends in her new classroom setting. In September we must begin anew as a whole class to create together an atmosphere that will nurture our growth and being.

Students and teacher alike share a relationship which is composed of reciprocal dispositions: emotions, feelings and moods. These dispositions towards each other build the atmosphere of the classroom. One side of the relationship is the emotional disposition of the child toward the adult; the other, the corresponding disposition of the adult towards the child. (Bollnow, 1989, p. 9) It is difficult to separate the two sides of this double-sided relationship completely, as they appear to unite and blend together in the atmosphere created. (Bollnow, 1989, p. 9) In the next story I interpret our dispositions towards each other and I examine my response to the children's activities. The way I am present to my students, in part, is what creates the atmosphere of the classroom.

As there are no rules to abide by in teaching, I find myself watching in a tentative manner so as not to close off or judge a child before I see him or her fully.

Being in Each Other's Company

"Matt, can I have one?"
"Matt, what about me?"
"Please, Matt!"
"I'll give you fifty cents for one . . . Okay? Fifty cents?"
"Save me one, Matt!"

Whines, pleads, screams and laughter smother the sounds of the logging truck, called a crummy, which roars down the road carrying the whole class to the Mac Blo clear-cut logging site on Vancouver Island. Matthew has brought a package of chocolate cigarettes on the first field trip of the year in the first week of September. Arms stretch frantically, waving in the air towards Matthew—the hub of all the excitement and activity.

Do I stop this? No, they will be eaten in a few minutes. Still, what if this scene were observed by administration? It looks like chaos. But . . . we are free in the woods on a logging road. I am commiserating with my students on a crime of sorts—misconduct. I feel a sense of siding with the enemy. What is the forester wedged in the back of the crummy thinking? Does he think me to be a bad teacher? Does he think I don't have 'control'? What about the driver who looks at me in the rear-view mirror?

They are both smiling, my comrades. They know kids.

My student teacher leans towards me and whispers. Elena's voice is almost frantic as she asks, "What would I do in a situation like this? Should you stop them? I mean, what are **you** going to do?"

I pause and think about how to best answer this question. Only a year ago I might have felt that I had to have an answer that involved action on my part—knowing a way to 'handle' the situation. But maybe it doesn't require 'handling'. Maybe I'll just watch and see. . . .

I have been trying to apply a quasi-Taoist bit of wisdom in relating with my students: "Don't just do something. Stand there." It can calm my panic and fend off my immediate reactions. (Todd, 1991) All too often in the classroom I have burst in to 'help' in what appeared to be a children's fight, only to discover, with regret, that if I had hesitated just a few minutes longer I might have watched the children solve their own dispute amicably. A teacher who leaves children to settle their own problems is often thought to be educationally irresponsible by peers, parents and children alike. The question for me is knowing when to stand aside, knowing when **not** to do something in the classroom. Like the Tao, which translates as 'the way' or 'the road', when to act and when not to act cannot be defined, only discerned.

My student teacher's mouth is open and she is still looking at me for an answer. I turn to her, smile, and admit the truth. "I don't know," I say. Her jaw drops a centimetre lower. I think to myself, "I've lost her. Gone is the confidence. . . . Maybe."

I smile at the kids and giggle. This scene really is funny to watch. Elena and I both laugh.

I watch as my students hang the fags out of their mouths and shout to their friends several seats ahead, "Look, look at this." Zachary holds the cigarette between his thumb and first finger, European style, then switches to the corner of his mouth, a gangster before me.

Roland lets it dangle from his lower lip, a little moisture holds the paper in place. He looks seedy. Youth is his redemption. Within minutes they have succumbed to the delicious chocolatiness. The issue of discipline melts before me.

The corners of Cristina's mouth turn up into a smile as her eyes roll to the left. She looks up. "I'm saving mine till later," she says. Her eyes are glittering as she carefully stows the slim paper-wrapped chocolate cigarette into a special pocket in her backpack. She has a plan.

The day is filled with stops and starts: looking for and at animals; eating lunch at brookside; wading in and getting soaked; throwing stones and listening to them go plonk. The forester has some curriculum to cover: heavy equipment, public relations for clear cuts, its positive effects on the economy and wildlife and the importance of "trees forever," their slogan. The students have their own curriculum: gum tattoos, gathering forest souvenirs (pine cones, they call them, despite the lecture otherwise) and gorging themselves on chips in the crummy. Occasionally the two curricula overlap.

The day comes to a close. We wave our goodbyes to the driver and the forester, who are now Al and Chris to us, and we board the ferry. I look forward to the children exploring the ferry ride home with their new-found friends. Perhaps, at last, I can read my book. No, it is not to be. Cristina parks herself a few seats away, closer to a nursing mother than to me. I watch out of the corner of my eye. She has waited for this opportunity when all her peers have left. She digs the chocolate cigarette out from her backpack and looks over to be sure that I am watching and within earshot.

"Nice baby. How old is he?" Cristina asks, ensuring that the woman will look at her as she holds the cigarette dramatically between her middle fingers. Cristina is both gracious and nonchalant.

"Three months," the innocent mother responds, doing a double take on seeing the fag suspended from Cristina's moistened lower lip. "Are you smoking?" she asks.

"I just started this morning," Cristina answers without a trace of emotion, while riffling through her backpack for what might be matches. "It's not lit."

"That's good. It's not good for you, smoking . . . ," the woman's voice trails off as she bundles up the baby, lifting him to her other side, away from possible smoke.

Cristina taps the cigarette several times and examines the flattened end for traces of dangling tobacco. "Don't worry. You can't smoke in the ferry anymore," Cristina assures the mother. "It's against the law."

"But you're **not** going to smoke, not at your age, are you? Don't you think you're a little young?" I can see this mother has Cristina's best interests at heart but is naive in the ways of children.

"My teacher knows. It's okay," Cristina gestures to me, leaning back to allow the woman full view of the adult who would endorse her bad habits.

The mother gives me a long, steely glance. "I see. . . ." She appears to be trying to memorize my face for later identification, perhaps in a mug shot.

"It's okay, I don't inhale," Cristina continues. She takes the cigarette out of her mouth and holds it up to examine the brand name impressed on the side of the paper.

"You see, it's just chocolate." She smiles, peels the paper off and allows the chocolate to melt in her mouth while she turns to smile at me.

What I Learn from the Children

During the field trip we have enjoyed each other's company. I reflect and consider what happened between us to create the enjoyable atmosphere. We have become attuned towards each other from our shared dispositions; these dispositions make it possible for the children and me "to be open to each other and to the possibilities of risk-taking that growth requires" (Smith, 1993, p. 448). The students and I have created a foundation for learning and comfort with each other which will serve in the classroom.

As I reflect on the day, I think of Vandenberg's ideas of atmosphere as a "unitary whole" created by the relationship experienced and created reciprocally between student and teacher. (1975, p. 40) While Vandenberg describes the pupil's side and the teacher's side separately, I explore the dispositions of the teacher and student as they co-respond in light of the field trip experience in the story about Cristina and the chocolate cigarettes.

'Cheerfulness', the first of Bollnow's dispositions, means "an elevated mood that allows one to expand freely into an expanding world." (Vandenberg, 1975, p. 41) Cheerfulness in my students during the field trip takes the form of "whines, pleads, screams and laughter" brought on by the thrill of chocolate cigarettes that Matthew has brought. The competition for cigarettes, with the ensuing stretching and waving to gain attention, further heightens the excitement. I hesitate while looking on at what might be interpreted as chaos, as I remember my own fun as a child with candy cigarettes, wrapped in their adult-like cellophane packaging with the Camels label. Then, each cigarette offered an opportunity to flirt vicariously with dangers we considered exclusive to adulthood. How could I possibly stop their fun, remembering the joy that candy cigarettes provided me and my brother as children? I recognize the adult counterpart of cheerfulness in my own attitude towards my students with my "willingness to abide with [their] sudden fits of loud laughter, boisterous merriment, and other expressions of . . . [their] cheerfulness, for these are necessary . . . to their general well-being." (Vandenberg, 1975, pp. 46-47)

Unfortunately, sometimes, the children's "exuberant expressions" can be "interpreted as maliciously motivated" by teachers who lack cheerfulness themselves. (Vandenberg, 1975, pp. 46-47) My conscience is soothed as I examine my reasons for not calling a halt to the boisterousness of the children. Some teachers and administrators might describe the children's behavior as 'out of hand'. Beyond the watchful eye of the institution I suffer slight pangs of guilt that we are 'getting away with something', the children and I.

Will they run home and tell their parents? Will I be thought of as an irresponsible teacher by their parents and by my student teacher? Will my students think me as 'soft' on discipline? My fears are assuaged as I remember Vandenberg's comment that cheerfulness in adults appears as serenity, or "an inward calm related to the courage to be" [which is] ". . . different from a forced cheerfulness." (1975, p. 47) My serenity allows the world of children to expand joyfully. (Vandenberg, 1975, p. 47) It is my tolerance of the students' behavior, and my remembrance of my own childhood pleasures that bring us together in an open manner.

My worries are further allayed by Bollnow's (1989) words:

> Many seemingly senseless pranks or foolish activities that children engage in are really less harmful than some mistrusting child experts suggest, and may in fact contain valuable significance for the fundamental process of child development. Laughter, especially, is to be seen in its positive character. Wherever laughter freely erupts, there is breached the feeling of separation, of contrariness, of reluctance to participate. The child can do nothing else now but join in fellowship and communion. Pitiable, therefore, is the teacher who in his or her suspicion sees every instance of laughter as a sign of mischief. Such a teacher invites, rather than heads off, trouble. (p. 20)

I consider how the children experience the field trip and then make my decision to quietly enjoy their merriment. My enjoyment is best reflected in these words: "The pupil's cheerfulness is exuberant; the teacher's, sedate." (Vandenberg, 1975, p. 47)

My students try on their perceptions of adulthood, as they imitate different styles of smoking with the candy cigarettes. It is obvious that Cristina has carefully studied the behavior of adults as she depicts them with her cool demeanour and her planned strategy to unnerve the mother on the ferry. She feigns a degree of worldliness in her caricature, and she surprises me with her knowledge of health regulations. In these actions, she reveals her view of the adult world around her that she would not have disclosed as herself in the classroom. In role, Cristina is cool and sophisticated. Perhaps she looks forward to being an adult who would be treated with dignity and equality. It is this "impetus toward the future, toward being an adult" that Vandenberg (1975) refers to as "morningness." (p. 41) He describes "morningness" as the feeling that predominates childhood and youth, the feeling one has on an invigorating morning when one looks forward to what the day will bring. On the other hand, "Cheerfulness is the anticipatory openness to the world, but morningness is the anticipatory openness for the 'journey' to the 'future'. . . ." (Vandenberg, 1975, p. 41)

Cristina's behavior is amusing, and, at the same time, disconcerting, for I wonder if she will be lured to smoke, or is she repelled by those who do? I wonder if she will lie to me, too, or is the cigarette just a prop that encourages exaggeration? Does her teasing have any meaning beyond the pretending of children? With the cigarette, Cristina, the child, is transformed instantly to the adult, bestowed with the powers to deceive another adult. Is her smoking and sophisticated manner a rehearsal of one of many roles in life, some to be assumed and others to be discarded?

Cristina tries on adulthood with her cigarette prop. She attempts to 'fell the giants' of parental authority by outsmarting the nursing mother and having a poke at me, her teacher. She attempts to gain an equanimity with adults in a world controlled by them. She seeks to find out who she is.

I trust that Cristina will have many opportunities to make decisions about smoking and deceiving others along the way, as I trust that there will be someone there to help her sort out the best decision; I also trust that Cristina will learn ways of being treated with equality and dignity with others.

'Good-naturedness' or 'good humor' is the corresponding disposition in the adult. (Vandenberg, 1975,

p. 47) Good-naturedness "trusts in the possibilities of the present" and it "hardly looks ahead to the next class or next week, because of a confidence in both oneself and the world." (Vandenberg, 1975, p. 47) As a teacher, my "trust in the possibilities" allows me to carry on through the worst moments working with children so that I do not condemn a child who is momentarily in trouble. It would be easy to think to myself any number of possible consequences for the child's future, such as, "This one will be on drugs," or, "She'll be pregnant in a couple of years," or, "He'll be in jail soon." But it is too soon to say. Even at the worst of times, I try to start fresh again each day with a child's actions, and I think to myself, "You never know. We have many chances at life."

I recognize the children's need for their own 'curriculum': candy cigarettes rather than looking for deer on the road; licking and applying bubble gum tattoos versus identifying Douglas fir from cedar. I have the patience, experience and the span of time behind me to recognize, accept and be amused at the children's fleeting enthusiasms. A cheerful child expects good things to happen almost everywhere and constantly. "He [or she] is delighted by continuously new discoveries as he [or she] experiences the new qualities of things." (Vandenberg, 1975, p. 41) The children are in expectant joy throughout the day ´as they marvel over how far a boulder can be thrown, the depth of the brook, and whether there are fish in the stream.

When we begin to study forestry back in the school, I know that the students will have gleaned a lot from the field trip. What they will recall will not **just** be chocolate cigarettes, gum tattoos, and boulder tossing. I do not interfere on the field trip; instead, I decide to use my practice of "don't just do something, stand there." This is an attitude akin to patience, which "willingly lets

perceived things be what they are without hastily imposing one's preconceptions and conceptions upon them."
(Vandenberg, 1975, p. 47) I am patient that the children
will be interested in many things during the day as it
unfolds, as this is "expectancy" on the part of the student. Many will remember the devastated terrain; some
will retell the clear-cutting practices and how it creates
deciduous tree populations, and there will be those who
recall the sounds and actions of the heavy equipment.
But during the field trip I can be patient not to direct
their attention further. They are taking in a great deal. It
is patience that assures me that in time I can expect
that the students will take in what they can.

≈

At 'Meet the Teacher Night' I share Cristina's story
with her mother and stepfather. I want her mother and
step-father to know that I appreciate Cristina's sense of
humor, that I find her smart and likable. As a teacher, I
am taking a risk: Will her step-father be annoyed by her
mischief? Will her parents think of me as a reckless
teacher? Will I lose Cristina's trust by not asking her
permission first to tell the story to them?

I surmise from the physical distance between
Cristina and Jack, her step-father, and the slight sneer
on his face directed towards her, that he considers her to
be a nuisance. The mother has shared with me before
that "things were fine between Jack and me until
Cristina arrived and then. . . ."

Cristina is watching her step-father's reaction
closely, in particular, to this story. She rapidly shifts her
attention from teacher to mother to step-father as she
searches each face for traces of anger or acceptance.
"Will I get in trouble?" her uplifted eyes and tense mouth

seem to say. Cristina is no longer the cool sophisticate she portrayed on the ferry. Instead, she appears to be afraid of losing more than just her privileges at this point, for the stakes are great—she may lose the foundation of acceptance she has begun to build with Jack. I must convey my intentions to her with my expression, to put her at ease, and to let her know that I mean only to convey my enjoyment of her with this story. Cristina may be challenging this year, but I must see beyond her tantrums in class and her insults to other students to take in her vulnerability and admire her sense of humor. My encouraging looks directed towards her must be authentic and consistent with my intentions for her.

I am laughing at the humor of her planning while I tell her parents of her caricature of adult behaviors. My laughter helps initiate their acceptance of the humor of the situation. Together we enjoy Cristina's adventure—her mischief, her cleverness and her game of 'let's pretend' with an adult.

Cristina sees our enjoyment and joins in, supplying details I left out. Her interjections bring forth a new dimension as she reveals her sensitivity to the baby's mother's reaction. "You should have seen her face!" she says and acts it out for us. "And that's where I added the part about it not being legal to smoke. Remember, Jack, in the paper . . . ?" Cristina refers to an article they read together and indirectly points out that she remembered that moment shared with him.

Her mother and step-father are seeing her differently through my eyes—Cristina is humorous. Her teacher finds her smart and she likes her. Jack smiles. He likes her, too.

This telling may help Cristina's mother and stepdad accept Cristina as she is. I have witnessed it—it is not just them, their failing as parents to change her game playing. This **is** Cristina. For me, to teach is to search and discover what is unique and different about each child and to attempt to enhance this uniqueness.

As a teacher, I must always keep in mind what Cristina is and what she can become. Now, her attempts to gain attention from other students fail because she is often demanding and annoying with them, after which, she suffers the pain of exclusion. But my knowledge of Cristina is wider and more intimate than a view that merely focuses on her misbehaviour. I know that she feels alienated far from her grandparents, her language and her native customs in Central America. I know about her humor and her sensitivity. In other words, I have a "sense of the deeper and significant aspects of her life" that make Cristina unique. (van Manen, 1991, p. 95) In considering the possibilities for her future, I must listen, consider a variety of vantage points, and give her opportunities to explore her needs and interests in a caring and supportive atmosphere. It is when we explore and discover our uniqueness that we are at home with ourselves.

The classroom is more than a physical space; it refers to spaces where caring for children is nurtured. In this story our classroom is a field trip. The classroom should not limit our experience; instead it provides us with room to learn.

Elizabeth Stone writes about the value of imparting family stories in *Black Sheep and Kissing Cousins: How Our Family Stories Shape Us*. When Cristina hears her teacher tell her story to her parents it helps to define her, to tell her who she is. (Stone, 1988, p. 31) She hears something about the 'truth' of herself through the retelling of her pretending. She joins in with details herself, which help to "fasten [her] identity in place and keep it from floating off, slithering away, or losing its shape." (p. 34) To hear a description of her humor does not fix her in a rigid role but helps to "provide cohesiveness and a sense of belonging" to a family that loves and tolerates her. (p. 35) Furthermore, she knows her teacher accepts her and appreciates her sense of humor. She is acknowledged for her uniqueness—her true self.

As teachers, we take part in shaping children's ways of being, but there is a danger that we demand that they conform to our ideal, robbing them of their own ways. We must help children search for their own potential and leave room enough for them to find it.

Exploring and Expanding Our Home

If each child can learn about his or her uniqueness through self-exploration in the classroom, perhaps we can lead children to explore commonalities with the lives of others. The classroom must be made a safe place in order for students to expand their worlds. As a teacher, I enable my students' growth through using my own experience as a source to share with them. In the next story, my students are shocked by another student's seemingly callous behavior upon the death of her father the previous night. Through a lifetime of experience I have reached a maturity I can call upon to help my students understand the intricacies of life. My openness creates an atmosphere in which they can share their experiences of loss and examine their feelings. The silence brought on with each telling permits the children to hear that others have similar sorrows in their lives. The stillness allows each story to "linger on to invite reflection, reckoning, coming to terms with something that is deep and powerful." (van Manen, 1991, p. 185)

My students cluster in the hall at 8:30 as they always do, but they seem concerned about something and talk excitedly. "What's up?" I ask.

Leah begins but Aaron interrupts her, wanting to be the first to tell me. Their eyes are downcast as if they are betraying a confidence. "Amy, you know Amy, upstairs?"

We are interrupted by the buzzer and my students barrel in the door to begin the morning routines before coming to the carpet. They are all gossiping in small groups and having difficulty listening to each other's stories about new pets and last night's birthday cele-brations.

"Leah, you have something to share," I invite her to speak. Leah looks anxious. She rarely offers any infor-mation and hesitates before speaking.

"Well, . . . yeah." She tilts her head on one side to ask, "Is it true? I mean, Amy Remington's dad died last night and she's here at school. And she's not even crying. She's making jokes!" Leah is shocked. "Can that be?" she stammers.

My students search my face for an answer. I hesitate for a few seconds, wondering whether I am breaching some unwritten school policy about speaking candidly of reactions to death. Yet, I have something to offer them from my experience that may prove to be worthwhile for them. Perhaps I can let them understand that Amy is not bad; our reactions to death are not always what we think they will be.

I begin slowly, "Sometimes people act strangely when someone they love dies or is near death."

I pause again to reflect on my choice of words and my willingness to dig into my own memories. The room is hushed and every eye is on me. They know there's more to come and I won't let them down.

"Twenty-one years ago my mother had a stroke," I barely get the words out before the questions begin.

"What's a stroke?" five or six children call out.

"Oh, it's when a blood clot stops the oxygen from getting to your brain," Perry helps out.

"Ooohhh," they murmur in chorus and urge me to continue.

"'You can't expect her to make it,' the neurosurgeons told me." "'They don't come out of comas.'" I laugh to myself, "I almost threw her false teeth out when they told me that." My students don't get it.

"I went grocery shopping after they told me, pretending that everything was normal. . . . And the way I reacted to that news was . . ." I falter a bit here, before going on, "I rammed my cart into an old, grey-haired lady in the supermarket . . . on purpose."

I look at my students' reactions. They don't gasp as my adult friends have done when I tell them this. "Then I screamed at her, 'Why are you alive when my mother's not!'"

My students are still, held fast by my story and my open show of emotion. Frowns appear and eyebrows quiver. My students do not question, nor do they judge; they accept my experience. They hear how it is with me and say what they must, too. Stories begin to trickle.

Bradley begins, "My little brother, he was three months, when he died. But I didn't cry. Not at all. My mom, she cried all the time. She cried all day and all night. That's all she did was cry." We are all snug, listening deeply, breathing as one.

"I didn't say nothing. I didn't feel anything," Bradley's voice sounds puzzled. "All I said was, 'Gee, mom, that's too bad.' I didn't even cry. I never cried."

Bradley is new to my class this year. The only exchanges we have had are those that deal with his math accuracy and his acute observations in class. But I do know from what he shares in class that at home Bradley does not hold the rights to his own feelings, his mother has the deed. She tells him how to feel, "You should . . ." and "You're wrong to feel that way." The classroom is the place where Bradley can hear how others react and where he can reflect on his own experiences.

We are quiet for a while, entering into the privacy of our own stories, respecting Bradley's. Silence is the only appropriate response here—it is "the tact of the 'silent conversation' where chatter would be misplaced, or where intrusive questions may only disturb or hurt." (van Manen, 1991, p. 177) The children show each other the same sensitivity. We are listening for the "undertones" of our inner lives which can only be heard in silence. (van Manen, 1991, p. 173)

Without raising her hand, Amber begins. "When my little brother, he died of cancer, he was four, there were all these **people** in the house," Amber spits out the word "people". I thought they'd never leave. They were relatives, but I never saw them before. They were there **all** the time. **All** the time. And I just wanted to say, 'Would you just **leave**!'"

I don't respond in words to their stories. To listen seems just right. It is that "granting of silence that leaves space for the child to come to him-or herself." (van Manen, 1991, p. 177) It is not just the absence of our talk that marks this silence. "Rather, it is the silence of patiently waiting, being there, while sustaining an expectant, open, and trusting atmosphere." (van Manen, 1991, p. 177)

The hush does not last long. Amber's story has made me think of a moment long ago. "When the ambulance came for my mom the neighbours all came for blocks. They took her out on the stretcher. She wasn't my mom anymore . . . not to them. She was an **event**," I punch this last word, aware of my anger for the first with dignity and equality. It is this "impetus toward the future, toward being an adult" that Vandenberg (1975) refers to as "morningness." (p. 41) He describes "morningness" as the feeling that predominates childhood and youth, the feeling one has on an invigorating morning when one looks forward to what the day will bring. On the other hand, "Cheerfulness is the anticipatory openness to the world, but morningness is the anticipatory openness for the 'journey' to the 'future'. . . ." (Vandenberg, 1975, p. 41)

Cristina's behavior is amusing, and, at the same time, disconcerting, for I wonder if she will be lured to smoke, or is she repelled by those who do? I wonder if she will lie to me, too, or is the cigarette just a prop that encourages exaggeration? Does her teasing have any meaning beyond the pretending of children? With the cigarette, Cristina, the child, is transformed instantly to the adult, bestowed with the powers to deceive another adult. Is her smoking and sophisticated manner a rehearsal of one of many roles in life, some to be assumed and others to be discarded?

Cristina tries on adulthood with her cigarette prop. She attempts to 'fell the giants' of parental authority by outsmarting the nursing mother and having a poke at me, her teacher. She attempts to gain an equanimity with adults in a world controlled by them. She seeks to find out who she is.

I trust that Cristina will have many opportunities to make decisions about smoking and deceiving others along the way, as I trust that there will be someone there to help her sort out the best decision; I also trust that Cristina will learn ways of being treated with equality and dignity with others.

'Good-naturedness' or 'good humor' is the corresponding disposition in the adult. (Vandenberg, 1975,

p. 47) Good-naturedness "trusts in the possibilities of the present" and it "hardly looks ahead to the next class or next week, because of a confidence in both oneself and the world." (Vandenberg, 1975, p. 47) As a teacher, my "trust in the possibilities" allows me to carry on through the worst moments working with children so that I do not condemn a child who is momentarily in trouble. It would be easy to think to myself any number of possible consequences for the child's future, such as, "This one will be on drugs," or, "She'll be pregnant in a couple of years," or, "He'll be in jail soon." But it is too soon to say. Even at the worst of times, I try to start fresh again each day with a child's actions, and I think to myself, "You never know. We have many chances at life."

I recognize the children's need for their own 'curriculum': candy cigarettes rather than looking for deer on the road; licking and applying bubble gum tattoos versus identifying Douglas fir from cedar. I have the patience, experience and the span of time behind me to recognize, accept and be amused at the children's fleeting enthusiasms. A cheerful child expects good things to happen almost everywhere and constantly. "He [or she] is delighted by continuously new discoveries as he [or she] experiences the new qualities of things." (Vandenberg, 1975, p. 41) The children are in expectant joy throughout the day ´as they marvel over how far a boulder can be thrown, the depth of the brook, and whether there are fish in the stream.

When we begin to study forestry back in the school, I know that the students will have gleaned a lot from the field trip. What they will recall will not **just** be chocolate cigarettes, gum tattoos, and boulder tossing. I do not interfere on the field trip; instead, I decide to use my practice of "don't just do something, stand there." This is an attitude akin to patience, which "willingly lets time after all these years. "Just entertainment for the crowd. They hung around after the ambulance drove off, discussing what they'd watch next. I was left with my rage, witness to my mother stripped of her dignity." My students may not understand my last words but they know my feelings.

We have been on the carpet for a long time yet no one is fidgety. Each of us is locked in personal reverie. Amber has more to say. "When he died, my brother, they took away his furniture in his room. We shared that room," she rails, "that was my room, too. The bunk, I **loved** that bunk bed, the desk, the book case . . . everything. They took it all away." Her voice trails off and Amber moves from being wistful to being furious. "Nobody even asked me. It was like . . . they had to get rid of everything that was his. And I had nothing, **nothing** left of him. It was **then** my parents split up." Amber is clearly angry about her powerlessness over the loss of a brother, her furniture, her privacy, and then her parents. Three years have passed since his death. For her, this is the first year to talk about it with her peers.

Andrea is Amber's best friend and she begins, "When my cat died, at the vets, they put her to sleep, you know," she informs us. "She was a really nice cat. Everybody loved her. My dad, he called my mom. My mom couldn't stop crying. I don't know why. She didn't even **know** the cat. They had split up, so she couldn't have even known the cat. We all went to the vet. All of us, we went to the vets. All of us except Jenny, my sister. Nobody came and got Jenny in school. She was really mad. Jenny's still mad, when we talk about it. And my mom cried more than any of us."

The stories flow now. Hands are up everywhere on the carpet. Adam, with his unusual abilities, is often isolated. He has a slow way of speaking that makes other students lose interest. But that is not the case today. A deep frown grows across his forehead and his eyes appear clouded as he begins, "My mom, she had a sister . . . my aunt, she would've been. But she died a long time ago . . . so I never got to know her . . . before I was born."

I look at Adam and say, "You're wondering what she might have been like . . . ?"

"Yeah," Adam sighs a little.

"Maybe even . . . if she might have been like you . . . ?"

Adam's eyes brighten and he cocks his head slightly to one side and nods, "Yeah. . . ."

I smile, as I know of Adam's loneliness, "Maybe she would have liked you. . . ."

"Yeah!" he agrees, smiling wide.

I have established contact with Adam; my caring glance has conveyed my understanding to him. (van Manen, 1991, p. 173) I have sought his feelings and found them in his expression.

John is a new boy in my class this year. Each day he forces his doughy body into grey sweatpants that ripple around his middle. John tells me he has never lived any place for more than two years, because his father gets laid off or "he doesn't get along with his boss" or "they can't afford to pay the rent." "We just keep moving," he laments to me in private.

Today he shares with the whole class, "My uncle, he died last week. He just **died**. His wife and kids went out to the movies and he stayed home and he died. In front of the t.v. In the lazyboy. All alone. There was nobody there. They came back and found him there. He died just like that." Each utterance is staccato—a fact not yet comprehended. John's voice is filled with disbelief that it could happen like this.

I am wondering if he is thinking, "If it could happen to my uncle, could it happen to **my** family, too?" This is a moment when it is more important for me to hold back my inferences. John needs the privacy to ponder these thoughts so new to him.

Everyone has a story about death. Dead pets. Grandparents. The man in the co-op with AIDS. The lady with cancer. The interest of the children does not wane with the stories of others. Each story releases another telling. Some seem to trigger others.

"Can we change the subject? I don't want to talk about this any more." Stephanie makes a quick suggestion through all her orthodontistry, "Can we do the Clue box?" I don't probe Stephanie's reasons.

"No, not yet," a few voices persist. For them, there is more to say and hear now.

"Yes, the Clue Box," most of the voices agree. "Michelle's turn. Who will be the recorder?"

"I will, I will," voices ring out. And the rhythm of the classroom changes.

The classroom provides me with the constant challenge of allowing for and responding to each unanticipated situation. When to begin a discussion? Which discussion to pursue? When to end? How to respond? First, we must see the "pedagogical possibilities in ordinary incidents." (van Manen, 1991, p. 187) The other part of the answer lies in what the students and I have done jointly; our sensitive responses to each other have determined the significance of our discussion. (van Manen, 1991, p. 187)

We have opened up a subject of vital concern, that, for some, may be a first-time opportunity to examine their feelings about death and loss, let alone hear those concerns voiced by their peers. In the way that I treat their experiences as valid, I acknowledge that the chil-

dren have complete feelings and experiences. They come
to value their own experience by being heard in an atmosphere of safety. What had been an incident is converted
into a significant moment through our sensitivity to one
another. This is what it is to be 'at home' in the classroom, to extend the walls of the classroom and go
beyond its boundaries to explore the world in safety and
comfort.

What the Children Learn from Me

In each of the stories so far, I related how the atmosphere the students and I create in the classroom in
being with each other has an effect on them. Yet, I have
not given much mention to how the children have created a home for me. My next story tells how my students have transforming effects on my professional and
personal life. They demonstrate their capacity for
remarkable caring with me when I return to school after
the death of my mother. Their sensitive actions transform me because it allows me to be taken care of by my
students, instead of my being their caregiver.

This is my first day back at school, a Monday, after
my mother's death. Evan is the first to arrive each morning. He waits in the hall with the security of knowing
that his close friends, Rollie, Zachary and Perry will show
up within minutes to run the boardwalk together. They
run together. They are solid friends.

"We've formed a club, Ms. Sinclaire," Perry
announced last week.

"Yeah, we're the Flying Demons," Zachary informed
me without a trace of embarrassment.

But this morning the moments of waiting for his
friends' arrival are long for Evan. Alone, without his
friends, he is embarrassed to see me in the hall. There is
an expression of discomfort on his face. I read it to say,

"Oh, oh. What if she cries?" Evan wants to look at me, but without meeting my eyes. I sense his discomfort and smile. I cannot be inauthentic, especially now, for I do not have the strength. I greet him, "Hi, how are you doing?"

Evan nods, wordless.

"It's nice to be back." His face melts into relief.

As I round the corner to head for the photocopier I recognize Rollie's and Perry's voices. "Teacher's back!" I hear Evan half-whisper. Even his whisper is high-pitched and excited. "She's okay. . . ." The message ends with a rising intonation.

"Goooooood," Rollie and Perry sigh. They want their teacher to be normal.

Ten minutes later I return to the hallway. I want the students to know I am there and all in one piece.

"Here she comes," says Aaron. He always wants to be the first to tell. Stephanie and Michelle, Elizabeth, Brittany and Bianca are there. They look stiff and watch me nervously.

"Hi, I missed you guys," I say. They look at me indirectly and have difficulty finding words. I wonder how we will get through this period. I wonder how I can be strong for them; what will I do if I cry and, if I do, how will they react? We all seem distant from each other, like friends who, after an absence, don't know if they will like each other any more.

It is Monday morning and that means gym time first thing up. The children are obviously relieved to head to the big, cavernous gymnasium which allows for a great space between us all. They choose to play octopus, but I notice a hanging back, a reserve, amongst many of the students. Every few minutes a child drops out and comes to sit within a few feet of me. First, Amber.

"I'm just a little tired," she says, fanning her face with her hand, moving a few inches closer with every few minutes.

I smile at her. She returns a wider smile, with a giggle and returns to the game. Danielle and Nadine come together "to catch our breath." Danielle slips her fingers inside my bent elbow. I look at her and smile. Both skip back to the game. The time seems to pass so slowly.

Should I be doing something? Supervising this game? No, they're okay. I am uncomfortable with their discomfort and tentativeness. I wish I could reassure them that their teacher is back and that I am okay but my words alone would not convince them.

We return to class and sit together uncomfortably on the carpet. My students want to fill the quiet with the usual noise and jokes, but they cannot find the words, so I begin: "Thank you for the nice cards and let-ter you left me. I missed you all a lot when I was away." I hesitate, ". . . I want you to know that I may not be myself for a little while, and . . . I might even cry, but that's not unusual for you to see."

"Yeah," Aaron chimes in, easing the tension, "You even cried in that elephant book, *The Incredible Jumbo.*" All the kids laugh at my sentimentality and I do, too.

I wait a moment and continue, "When somebody you love a lot dies you remember things at different times . . . you never know when . . . and sometimes you cry. I might do that. It'll get better and I'll be myself again. Okay?" I ask their permission.

"Okay," they all mumble and nod softly in some kind of informal agreement. No one disagrees or sneers at my fragility. My vulnerability opens up human truths and my students are touched by it.

It's 3:15 on the same day and Kacey, Cassandra, Leah and Melisa are all hanging around inside the classroom, talking softly. "Can we **help** you?" Kacey whines, with her head on one side, her hair covering the other half of her face.

"Yeah, can we?" Leah joins in, "We could do your cupboards."

I shake my head with a late day, tired smile, trying hard to be strong.

"Are you **sure**?" Cassandra stretches out the "sure" part of the question. They surround my desk and talk about their solo acts for the upcoming concert and what our music teacher, Mr. Gray, says needs polishing. Kacey tells me about her brother's hockey team weekend getaway while Leah complains that she wishes she had a brother so she could get away too. Cassandra joins in with all the reasons why Leah really wouldn't want a brother. She's got one—she knows. The girls are getting closer to my chair all the time, I notice, until Kacey and Melisa are pressing on my body. Kacey's words are idle chatter, but her eyes look longingly at me, as though she were searching for my pain. I smile at her but the corners of my mouth twitch and my eyes form tears I'd hoped to hide from my students.

Kacey quickly puts her arm around me and hugs me. "Oh, Ms. Sinclaire. . . ." She continues to stroke my arm as she chatters about her little sister getting stuck in the motel toilet, as though all the talk will put me at ease. It fills up the silence.

I grin at the girls and tell them they'd better leave. They are satisfied only when I chase them out. The students hope that I will be restored to my former self, the person who helps to create the 'homey' feeling of the classroom through laughter and honesty.

In the classroom we have created an atmosphere of openness towards one another which enables the children to care for me when I most need it. For two weeks they hang around to 'help' after school, to welcome me 'home' again, until my laughter returns.

4

Becoming at Home in the World

Making a Home for All

There are situations in the classroom which allow children to grow when they are required to make ethical and moral choices, to exercise decisions and to take responsibility. In this chapter, I show how the growth required of them in making these choices expands their world beyond the classroom, beyond their immediate community, in such a way that they begin to take greater responsibilities for each other and their home in the world in which they live. In one situation, after a short but poignant read-aloud about cheating, everyone, including me, has a confession to offer about stealing. These situations require my attunement so that I can elaborate and extend our discussions long enough for the children to see the choices they have made, and then to reflect on their actions.

When I become honest about my experiences, not just my successes, but my failures, my mistaken decisions and my resulting disappointments, my students find value in my stories. Rather than judge me harshly, they use what they can from my experiences to sort out their own ideas and steer their way through somewhat more charted territories.

One such situation is described in the next story. I recount what happens in class after I read aloud a short story about two boys who plot to cheat the local junk man. The children in my class confess their own thefts and I take the risk to admit that I, too, stole as a teenager. Thereby, I remain genuine and keep my personal relationship with my students. Sharing my own experiences and admitting my own mistakes with the children allows them the same freedom to unburden themselves. My classroom can provide a home for honest discussion.

Have you ever made one of those mistakes that they warn you against in your teacher training? You're told, "Always preview a film before showing it to the students" or, "Always have your focusing questions ready before the students listen or observe." And then there's the proverbial, "Never, never, ever read a book aloud to your class before you've read it." That's the one I transgressed.

We were all enjoying the comfort of close companionship together on the carpet after sharing. The children and I wanted to extend that feeling a little longer with a read aloud selection.

"Less work," retorts Andrea with an impish grin.

"I'll read another one from *Soup* then," I say.

"Yeah, *Soup*, that'll be good," pipe up Aaron and Paul.

Both the boys and the girls like the short stories in *Soup* by Robert Newton Peck (1974) despite their depiction of a time well before the birth of their own parents, a time when Saturday afternoon matinees were called picture shows and their admission price was a dime.

A few of the stories have plots that are so simple that the children ask at the end, "Is that all?" or they respond, "So what? I don't get it." Afterwards we discuss the extraordinary qualities of ordinary occurrences. I begin to notice that the topics of the children's discussion and writing become concerned with the little moments in their own everyday lives. The *Soup* stories and our ensuing discussions and writing have slowed time down enough to allow us to linger in an appreciation of the sacred quality of the mundane in our own lives.

The main characters in *Soup* are two boys: Soup is the mischievous one and Rob, the narrator and straight man. Rob has a conscience in most matters but can be influenced by his friend, and each time he must suffer the consequences. All the students, girls and boys alike, know someone like Soup, a daredevil, a risk taker, a good kid who tests the limits and crosses over to the other side only to get caught. A few identify with Soup but most with Rob.

I started with reading "Cheating Mr. Diskin." (Peck, R.N., 1974 pp. 41-48) The title hooked our attention immediately. The two main characters each need a dime to go to the double bill: Laurel and Hardy and a singing cowboy film. To earn the money, they collect tin foil and turn in it in to the junk dealer. But Soup has an idea that they should cheat Mr. Diskin by adding a pebble to the foil ball to ensure they will have sufficient weight to receive a dime. Rob doesn't want to. "It's wrong, Soup. Let's not do it" he says, but faced with the threat of missing the show and being too far from home to ask his mother for a few pennies, he submits. (p. 43)

And there it is, at the top of the freshly turned page, a teacher's nightmare, glaring at me as I read aloud. I halt at the word 'Jew' and quickly edit out Soup's excuses for cheating the junk dealer, "it wasn't really so bad to cheat a Jew" and "I heard that guy say that there was no such thing as a good Jew." (p. 44) My principal suggested this book. I know it is on the shelves of many libraries, and, therefore, has some seal of approval. My students have little contact with Jewish people, though, and I don't want to leave them with any misconceptions. My reading becomes choppy and falters.

"What is it, Ms. Sinclaire?" Bradley asks, as his eyebrows wrinkle.

Quickly I cut to the part where the boys stuff the pebble in the wad of tinfoil and wrap it into its original cabbage shape. My students listen with interest to the proceedings. "Mr. Diskin is nice, they shouldn't" is written all over Kristjana's face. Her hands form tight little fists as she listens to the description of Mr. Diskin's smile and his ritualized way of greeting the boys. Each time he weighs their tinfoil with a handkerchief wrapped around his eyes and the scales in his hand, as if to mimic blind justice.

We get to the line that describes Mr. Diskin going in to his shack to get the dimes, "He was gone longer than usual," when there is a prickle of nervousness in the classroom. (p. 46) The students sense that Soup and Rob will not get away with it.

On returning from his shed, Mr. Diskin hands the boys two dimes and the stone they hid inside their ball of foil. He is not wearing his customary smile and his head shakes back and forth as if to say no. The story ends with the boys agreeing that they feel "like a hunk of dirt." (p. 47)

"That's stupid!" shouts out Kristjana, outraged. "Why did he give them the money if they cheated him?"

The children look at me, as if to expect an answer. "What do you think?" I ask them.

Evan knows and he leans forward in the direction of Kristjana, not me, and says, "To teach them a lesson. Because if he gave them the money then they'd feel worse."

"Oooohhh," comes from Kristjana.

Paul talks quietly to his friend, Aaron, about why Rob and Soup don't go in and steal all the dimes in his shed. Paul never shares anything controversial in class. He often warns his friends, Rollie and Aaron, who divulge their evening adventures of sneaking into private parking lots to examine luxury cars, "Don't tell her. She'll call your parents!"

Now the children talk amongst themselves for a few minutes. They don't seem to want to leave this topic alone. Something further is demanded of me that requires that I act upon the spur of the moment. All the theories I have learned and information I have read do not help me at this moment. It seems important to let the children have their say in the midst of their peers because it is here, in the classroom, in the stories we tell each other about ourselves, that we connect ourselves to a common thread of humanity. It is in these discussions that we teachers help each child determine what is right and wrong, not just for his or her own family, friends or community, but for all who inhabit our greater home on earth.

Perry begins, "Sometimes me and Matthew, we go to Toys R Kids, you know, and when the store owner's not looking . . . we use the candy machine. Oh, we put money in but we keep turning the handle and more candy keeps coming out."

"He gets really mad!" Matthew joins in shaking his head and rolling his eyes, "the store owner. He's not nice."

"Yeah, he's Chinese," Perry adds.

"Chinese?" I ask.

"Yeah, so it's not like . . . it really matters," Aaron adds.

"I do it, too. But I put in pennies when you're supposed to put in nickels." "Boy, does he get mad!" Evan says indignantly. "One time he caught me and opened up the machine. All the kids do it. They all put in pennies."

"So . . . because he's Chinese, it's okay?" I ask. The students cast their eyes downwards out of view. Their heads wiggle like bobbing dogs in the back seat of cars, not yes, not no. The children need to see their moral responsibility to all the members of their community, whether they know them or not.

"Well, it's still cheating . . . but. . . ."

"But because he's different from you, it's okay?" I press on.

"No, I guess it's not. But he gets so mad at us!"

Why, I wonder, did I leave out the part about Mr. Diskin being a Jew? This is another case of 'us and them', insider and outsider. The Chinese merchant is not part of their community, therefore he is an easy target as the children see it. Yet the children find their own justification for theft—the merchant's bad temper. What do I do? What do I say? Do I moralize at this point? Which should I address first—racism or theft? van Manen (1991) helps to shed some light on my quandary:

> Pedagogical action and reflection consist in constantly distinguishing between what is good or appropriate and what is not good or less appropriate for a particular child or group of children. In other words, pedagogical life is the ongoing practice of interpretive thinking and acting—on the part of adults, but also and especially on the part of the children who continually interpret their own lives and who constantly form their own understandings of what it means to grow up in this world. This does not imply, of course, that every single thing we say and do with children places us in a situation of moral choice. But it does mean that our living with

children is oriented in certain directions and that, as adults, we are accountable with regard to the reasonableness or goodness of our influencing of children. (p. 60)

In being with the children I see the need for them to examine their actions and choices, as mature people do.

"I stole too, you know," I say. Everyone's listening. "Not when I was a kid but when I was a teenager. We didn't have much money, no allowance. . . ."

"No allowance!" a chorus of voices rings out.

"No, no allowance. My parents said they couldn't afford it. 'What do you need money for anyways?' my dad always said. And I was too young to get a job. So my friend and I heard some kids were shoplifting and we decided to try it. We were nervous but it was exciting, exhilarating, in fact. We did it all summer. Shorts, tops, blouses—I even got two blouses that were the same. I don't know if my mother caught on, she didn't say. I guess I thought I could just lie to her and get away with it."

All the students are riveted at hearing this admission from their teacher. The situation has called for me to share something of myself that will contribute to the "children's well-being, growth, maturity and development." (van Manen, 1991, p.28) What I offer must be something that allows them to examine their own experiences. Here, in our classroom community, the children create a safe home to reflect on their thoughts and actions, make decisions and take responsibility in the future in the outside community.

I feel that I must take this risk and tell my students my story, despite whatever jeopardy it may put me in. I must risk the possibility that they may go home and tell their parents, who may, in turn, call the principal or the board. All may deem me unfit to teach children. Yet, only by taking this kind of risk do I attain what I consider to be educational success. (Bollnow, 1971, p. 529) I must trust my students by telling them of my own mistakes, for inherent is my message, "I made a mistake, I changed. So can you. We can go on from here." It is worth the risk for it is my ethical responsibility. It follows that the failure of my risk weighs heavier, for, if in my openness, I fail to convey my message of hope to my students, I will have failed. I have to weigh the value of the risk: if we succeed, my involvement is considered worthwhile by others; whereas, if I fail then I may appear to be "the one who had lacked necessary precaution, one who had acted with irresponsible credulity and stupidity." (Bollnow, 1971, p. 530) Then I "must bear ridicule as well as experience failure in . . . [my] work." (Bollnow, 1971, p. 530)

I continue to tell, "Fall was coming and I hated my winter coat. It had a foamy lining that the wind blew right through. In winter I got so cold I'd feel sick to my stomach. But I knew my parents wouldn't be buying me another one, so I decided to steal one. And I decided that if I was going to steal, I was going to steal 'big'—a suede coat with a fur lining, I had it all picked out. I planned it all—I think I liked that best, the planning. I made a map, a floor plan of where it was located; I had a recent department store box; I knew how to rip the tag in half to make it look like it was sold; I knew where I could stash the coat without a clerk seeing me in a mirror. That was before cameras."

"Well, did you?" My students are eager to know if I got away with it.

"Yes, I carried it right out of Eaton's with my heart beating like a symphony drum. That's when I made my mistake. Helga, my friend with me, decided she wanted some stuff from Woodward's. My plan was to stash the box where you can check parcels in and then go with her. Just in case. . . ."

". . . you got caught," Stephanie finishes the sentence off for me.

"Mmmhmmm," I nod. "But I didn't . . . I didn't check the box in," I repeat. "I carried it around. Well, . . . Helga got greedy. She was trying things on in the dressing room and stuffing things in without even thinking about whether she was being watched. So was I. We were overly tired and we took the escalator out. We were grabbed by two store detectives who took us to the freight elevators. I'll never forget that grip she had on me. I don't remember anything en route to the elevator. Everything was a blur. Before, I was getting away with it, then I was smart but when I was caught, I was stupid and somehow . . . dirty, like the boys in *Soup* (1974, p. 46) who say, they feel like 'hunks of dirt'. So did I."

I decide to hold nothing back from my students. They will hear the story of what happened and they will hear it from the 'inside out'—the way I felt it at the time. To hear how I experienced the shame is crucial to their understanding of how stealing changes everything. Telling my students what I did means allowing myself to be very vulnerable in going back to memories that I haven't visited for many years. I am entrusting thoughts and feelings to my students that I have never spoken about to anyone. I cannot merely 'pretend' to trust. I must give my trust completely or I will not appear to be considered to be trustworthy by my students. (Bollnow, 1971, p. 531)

It is worth the risk because it means it may bring things "within reach of [my] students that they never would have gained by themselves." (Bollnow, 1971, p. 533) At the same time, my fate lies in the hands of my students because I open myself up to them. (Bollnow, 1971, p. 533)

The students wait a moment before they start in with questions. "Well, what happened?" Brittany asks.

"These men in suits asked a lot of questions and then the police came. They were more fun and Helga and I relaxed a bit until they said they were taking us 'downtown'—to the police station, and then they'd drive us home."

"'It's okay,' I said, 'We could get home on our own.' The police looked at each other and smiled. Then they took us to the police station and asked us a lot of questions in a grey cement room with lines painted on the floor. One detective sprang up at a certain point and said, 'Okay, we've heard enough. Let's take 'em home.'"

"Well, that's when Helga and I got anxious. If my mom was home, it would be bad. She'd be ashamed of me. But if my dad was home, it would be terrible. Who knows what would happen? Yelling, maybe even hitting me. I had to get out of this somehow. 'It's okay, we can take the bus,' I told the detectives."

"'No, taking you girls home is just routine,' one said."

"I waited a while and then I tried again. 'Nobody's home and I have to stop and get some things.' They just shook their heads and smiled. We were coming up the block where our house was and I whined, 'Just let me off on the corner.'"

"'Sorry,' the other detective said and laughed. Both walked me right up to the door and knocked. It was 3:30. My dad wouldn't be home until 5:30. But it was my dad who opened the door."

"'How come you're home?' I asked. Shock was written all over my face and I felt sick."

"'Knocked it off early after doing some work at the airport. What's going on here?' he demanded."

"I don't remember what was said. But enough that there was nothing more for me to explain. I expected the yelling to begin, but instead my father said quietly, 'You'd better go to your room for a while.' That's when I started bawling."

I look up and into the distance, away from my students who are listening, as I recognize that incident to be a turning point in my relationship with my parents. "You know, they never really trusted me again after that. There was a distance. I wasn't a child anymore; I wasn't an adult either. But we were never as comfortable with each other again. Something was gone forever. Lost."

A thoughtfulness takes over the mood of the classroom and we become quiet. We are snug in our blanket of confidentiality. In my candid admissions, I have left the "throne of perfection, and by this act, [I have] acknowledged an ultimate equality with [my] students, removing the usual teacher-student relationship." (Bollnow, 1971, p. 534) Bollnow (1971) says that in these situations:

> The student feels himself elevated by this acknowledgment and the teacher has lost nothing in the eyes of his student. Furthermore, the teacher has gained something, for by deciding to overcome himself, he has gained greater respect from all his students. (p. 534)

Rollie begins, "I took this transformer from Toys R Kids. I don't know why. I liked it, I guess. I never played with it though, I felt so bad. My dad, he knew. He knew I didn't have the money and he made me take it back. It was soooo embarrassing. I thought I'd die. The store owner was nice though. My dad, he offered to buy it for me. I didn't know what to say and so I didn't say anything. He bought it and I've still got the package in my desk. I've never opened it. I always feel so bad when I see it there."

Amber drops her lids as she starts, "When I was at the beach last year, Jericho Beach, no, Kits, there was this man. He was lying on a towel and his stuff was all around him and there was $8.00 not too far from him. So I thought it might have been his, but I wasn't sure. But then it might not have been his. So I waited and nobody came along for the $8.00. So he went down to the water and when he left I walked over and bent down to make it look like I was looking for something." She giggles and looks at me askance, and says, "I didn't want anybody to know, you know . . . that I was . . . well, not stealing, just taking something that wasn't mine. And I held on to that money all afternoon in my pack. I thought about all the stuff I could buy, chips, ice cream. . . . I really wanted to. And then it was time to go home and the man was looking all over for something that was lost and I could see him. I felt sorry for him," she says, hanging her head on one side as her long bangs cascade over the one eye. She fastens her eyes on me behind the curtain of hair, as she continues, "But I kept hoping that I could keep the money."

"And finally, he comes over to my mom and me and he says, 'Did either of you see eight dollars? I had it out here.'"

"And I couldn't lie." There is disappointment in her voice as she says, "So I got it out of my pack and I gave it to him. My mom said she was so proud of me but I knew."

"Yeah, and you felt badly that he had to ask," I add. Amber nods.

The children continue to listen to each other and several hands are up to be next. Leah wants to know if it's stealing if you check telephone booths for change. "Is that the same as, like, Amber?" she asks, being careful not to cast blame on a fellow student who openly shared.

The class decides it's different because, as Stephanie says, "You don't know who the owner is, so it's okay. And even for Amber, she didn't really know until the end."

"Not for sure," Michelle adds.

"It's Aaron's turn," I interject.

"I went to the store for my mom. She sent me for some stuff and there was money left over, so I bought Nibs. I love them, the black ones. So does my mom. But it's not like she said, 'Oh, Aaron, if there's some change you can buy some candy for yourself.'" He mimics his mother's voice as he says this.

"So when I came back, my mom said, "Where's the change?'"

"I said, 'Here it is. But I didn't give her all the change 'cause I spent it on the licorice. Then I went to my room to eat the Nibs. Pretty soon my mom was at the door and she asked if she could have some licorice too.'"

I said, "How did you know?"

"She said, 'I saw it on your teeth, Aaron. Besides, you dropped a few. So can I have some?'"

"I reached in my pocket and it was all gone. I felt so bad. So she gave me some money and I went to the store and bought her some licorice. We ate it together and we laughed. She said, 'I'll bet you won't try that again.'"

More students tell stories and their interest doesn't wane. Francine tells a story of her dad who stole a leather jacket and never wore it. "It just hung in the closet and one day he decided he'd go back to the store and pay for it," she says.

All the stories contain remorse and a loss of trust and innocence. No one tells a story that glamorizes stealing. I wind things to a close and the children plead with me for "just a little more time."

"Tomorrow," I say, thinking that tomorrow will bring new concerns.

Paul, who is reluctant to share himself, says to Aaron, "Gee, that was really neat in sharing today."

This is at the vital heart of children's concerns. Something has happened here today in our confessions that has brought us closer. We have unburdened our mistakes; we will share that burden with each other, and having done so, each individual weight is lighter. We have communed together in the sense of forming an intimate fellowship from the rapport that has developed. We listen, knowing that Perry's story or Amber's story is our story too. This time the children see themselves as part of a community with moral and ethical responsibilities to its members. My risk of openness has been worth it.

The next morning the buzzer goes and the children pour in the door, heaving their backpacks onto their desks. Allan marches in, "I've got more to say about that topic from yesterday. Remember?" He reminds me of my promise to continue today, "You said. . . ."

"Okay!" Allan puffs, sitting cross-legged on the carpet. He looks around at everybody on the carpet and asks, "Can I start?"

The students nod their approval.

"Okay. I have to say this. "My dad found this bag from Kaboodles in my room. It had two erasers and a pencil in it but it didn't have any paper in it—you know, the recipe?"

"Oh, the receipt?" Stephanie offers.

"Yeah, the **receipt**," Allan emphasizes. "Anyways, my dad asked me about it and I couldn't lie. I stole it."

"I was so embarrassed, I started crying. Then my dad, he told me about when he stole something too, a long time ago, when he was a kid."

"But, but, did you have to . . . ?" Rollie wants to pry the consequences out of Allan.

"Yep! He made me take it back and tell the Kaboodles guy I was sorry. And I had to pay for it. I don't even like those erasers, they always remind me. . . ."

There's more stories. The children are squeezing out every last confession, perhaps in an attempt to start fresh again.

"I'm wondering if . . . it's ever okay to steal?" I ask, not with any particular moral goal in mind, just casting my line out to see what will bite.

"Oh, yeah, if your family's starving, that's okay," Stephanie is quick to answer, but then she hesitates, and says, "Well, maybe not okay . . . but not really bad."

"So there are degrees . . . ?" I ask.

"Yeah, like it's okay to steal, well, not steal, but . . . taste things at Safeway, like when you're buying grapes. Then, you see if they're okay, " Kristjana says, "I always do, even when I'm not going to buy any." Then she giggles.

A great rumble of chatter begins as tasting stories are shared with people seated on either side.

"Oh, Safeway!" Perry's sneering voice can be heard over the crowd. "I always go to the candies and try them like I'm going to buy a whole bunch. But I never do."

"It's okay?" I ask.

"Well, yeah, 'cause they make so much profit. They ask such high prices for everything. . . . It's just taking back something."

I wend my way through an explanation of how a company works, shareholders, employees to pay, expenses, the works. It's futile, though. The children don't see a company as living, breathing people with investments. For them, a company is a building that contains enormous fat men smoking cigars who get chauffeur-driven in limos. Many of the children agree that it's not cheating if it's a big company. For them, a company is not part of a community with people whose names you know and who know yours.

I find there comes a time in working with children when I have exhausted all my attempts to persuade them. I have said all that I can say. Perhaps the children need more life experiences, to work in the world, or for their parents to change their own attitudes and values. There is no more I can say so I do not press the issue further.

I pause to think about my own actions. I hesitate, for a teacher walks a thin line. I begin to say more. To have made a mistake in the past and admit it is shocking, but to admit that one cheats or even thinks about cheating today may not be acceptable to many. But I think it is important to understand a situation, in this case, stealing, from the perspective of the child in order to grasp his or her situation. I begin, "You know those bread tags, the ones that hold the plastic bag tight over the bread . . . ?"

My students nod.

"You know those supermarket carts where you have to put a quarter in to get to use the cart?"

They nod again.

I hesitate another moment. "I've heard that if you put one of those bread tags in, instead of a quarter you can get the cart . . . ?

Instantly Paul seizes the opportunity to consider the

financial possibilities. He asks, "You mean if you put a bread tag in, you could get a quarter out?"

Ever practical, Rollie answers, "No, I don't think so 'cause you just get out what you put in, so you'd just get back a bread tag."

"See!" Perry hisses, pointing his finger righteously at me and sitting up on his haunches, his head thrust forward, "You do it, too!"

I shake my head, "No, I only heard. . . ."

"Yeah, but you were thinking about it! You're no different from us!" His cheeks are puffed out and he is angry.

"Yeah," I admit, "I think about it. It bugs me to have to pay to use those carts even if I get the money back. Sometimes I don't have the exact change."

"Yes," I think to myself, "I am not really any different, older, more sophisticated, that's all." We are in the company of people we trust where we can consider our ethics, confess our sins, admit our mistakes and still be taken back into the fold. We have seen that others have erred and we have forgiven them. What's more, we have seen ourselves in each other and in the actions of others. We must, each and every one of us, then forgive ourselves so that we can make allowances for others. We are at home in each other's company and at home with ourselves. We are preparing to make our home in the world.

"Much education at home and even in schools takes place without conscious and deliberate planning," writes Max van Manen. (1991, p. 72) This story shows such an unplanned situation of growth in which the children benefit in some manner from the circumstances, and from my understanding and action. This is a situation in which the children can examine the decisions they make in their own lives and consider how their decisions affect others.

At times I receive confirmation of my efforts as an educator. The next story speaks of the development of children into moral beings, at home with themselves and others in the classroom. It tells of the rewards of my efforts over a period of time when they assume the cooperation, maturity, self-responsibility, and tolerance of each other. This story is etched out more sharply for me as I remember the same sense of awe I felt one morning in spring when I was present to see a natural occurrence while hiking.

Creating Their Own Home

Have you ever had an experience in nature that made you feel as though you had been blessed to be the one to be there to witness the miracle? Not a miracle really, just something that happens ordinarily in nature, but to those of us who live in cities who forget that such things take place within the earth each spring without our being there, at least a rare event. The only thing miraculous about it is that **you** were the privileged one to be there at that particular moment. I have a few memories of this quality that haunt me.

It was springtime and I was hiking up the side of a mountain along a long, slow, steep incline of a path. It stretched past tired patches of snow interspersed with the ooze of mud that comes from the sun filtering down through the canopy of trees to warm the soil and all its inhabitants below. That was the morning that hundreds, maybe thousands, of small mud covered frogs pulled their way out of the ground and slowly hopped across the path before me to make their way into the forest. They covered the ground so completely that there was no place to step. I could only stand and gaze at the sight. I have kept this image with me for over twenty years and I continue to marvel at what occurs unseen around us every day.

What reminded me again of this event was a scene as breathtaking and delicate that I witnessed when I entered the door to our classroom one morning. In the last story of the chapter I tell of when I discovered the students conducting their own morning meeting as I arrived late one morning.

The arrival bell to invite students to enter the school had rung at least ten minutes before, but I was caught in my own thoughts while photocopying behind the office door. I looked at my watch and I was startled, for I always try to be at the door to greet the children in the morning, in the same way my mother always waved to me from the kitchen window as I entered our back-yard after school. She'd hold the back door open to welcome me with her familiar smile that made me feel glad to be home. On this particular morning in the school, I raced down the stairs to my classroom, a little off-balance and swung the door open wide enough to allow room enough for me and all the materials I was carrying to enter.

All the students were on the carpet, quiet and con-ducting their own sharing time. Kristjana was seated in my little chair, posed just as I suppose I appear to my students when we do morning sharing. Her gestures were the same as, my own, right down to the hand move-ments. "Okay, Bradley," she said, "it's your turn after Perry. You can put your hand down until Perry finishes." She turned to him with a tactful smile to ensure that his feelings would not be hurt by her response.

For a few seconds the students did not notice me. During that brief time they waited their turn, as they might with me; they listened intently to each other with interest, and from their faces I noticed a few might have been preparing a question for the speaker. Then, at once, they all saw me standing there. They were startled by my presence. And I was ashamed to have interrupted what was theirs.

The children looked at me with shock, their eyes wide and mouths slightly open. "Oh, . . . I'm sorry, I just came in. I'm sorry to be late. . . ." I excused myself clumsily, "I've got to get something . . . I'll be back," and I stumbled my way back out the door.

By entering into this scene, just by virtue of my position I usurped the power for which I had prepared them. To be present during their meeting was to reinforce the imbalance that exists between us. It might have left them with the idea that their sharing was merely a rehearsal for the time when I would return to take over chairing the meeting. To leave the classroom may be considered to be renouncing my educational responsibility, yet to leave was in our best interests.

As I stepped outside our classroom door, I experienced mixed feelings at witnessing the delicacy of the moment: I felt the sadness of loss, for my students were not to need me as much again; I also felt a sense of pride from that loss, for I knew that I had prepared them well. Together the children and I have been creating a community in which they are learning to nurture and tend to each other's needs. They are able to respond to a classroom situation, make decisions and take responsibility. And some day soon, the larger community outside of the classroom will be their home to take charge of independently. They are becoming at home in the world.

5

The Stances of Teaching

Leading and Following the Children Home

Much of the time I find myself learning from my students, by being side by side with them in the classroom. In this chapter, I describe myself leading my students to new understandings through the different stances I take: by providing explanations and, at other times, by listening for what is missing from their knowledge in order to help them form a bigger picture for themselves. These stances I take to guide the children 'home'—to prepare them to become members of a larger community who shape the world around them. The stances are neither separate nor distinct, but often occur simultaneously. They stem from the relationship I have with my students; the stances play an important part in developing the atmosphere of the classroom. In the next story, I alternately lead and follow the children's understanding to help them create an understanding of others, themselves and the world.

It is read-aloud time and at last my students' chatter has subsided into a mood of quiet enjoyment as they snuggle together in the company of their familiar companions. As I look up from my reading to gaze at them, I feel a proud satisfaction. They have come so far since September when this time presented many difficulties:

"I don't wanna!"

"I don't like read-aloud!"

"That book's no good!"

"He's got my seat."

"Hey, I was sitting there!"

"Don't budge!"

"Is it almost over yet?"

Gradually over time the students become more patient and cooperative with each other; they risk more in their new-found security with me and each other; they show a curiosity and a frankness about the world that seemed initially hidden. I smile, believing that I am partly responsible for their growth and maturity.

"It's kind of boring," Aaron says, when I ask my third and fourth graders about their reaction to *The Best Christmas Pageant Ever* (Robinson, 1972), a popular children's story in which the cigar-smoking, foul-mouthed, bad-mannered Herdman children land all the parts in the church performance of the Nativity story. Rollie, Zachary and Stephanie nod their heads in agreement.

"Boring?" I think. It might have been the fact that we had just finished *The Indian in the cupboard* (Reid Banks, 1980), a fantasy-filled adventure, which they loved. But then I got to the part in *The Best Christmas Pageant Ever* (1972) that reveals the answer to me.

My students weren't getting the jokes. When they don't get the one about the 'swaddling clothes' which Claude Herdman mistakenly refers to as "wadded-up clothes," I stop and explain what swaddling clothes were, attempting to help them understand the meaning. But the 'swaddling clothes' are not an isolated fact they lack from the Nativity story, it is the Nativity story in its entirety. In the reading I stand as a bridge between my students' understanding and acquisition of a body of knowledge about the world and our traditions and culture. They can easily grasp the slapstick humor from the book; television provides that cultural reference. But because they are not familiar with the story of the birth of Jesus Christ they can not understand Imogene's indignant hollering about the oil as a shoddy gift from a king, "What kind of a cheap king hands out oil for a present? You get better presents from the firemen!" (p. 46)

Not unlike the Herdmans themselves, my students want to know who Herod was and why he was feared. When I explain Herod's decree to have all the babies under the age of two put to death as he was afraid for his own position, my class shrieks in chorus, "He can't do that!"

This opens discussion to the misuse of power and the fear that dictators have of being overthrown.

"That couldn't happen today," Allan, a third grader proudly announces.

"Couldn't it?" I ask. "Can you think of places where power is abused today? What happens there?"

A thoughtful look comes over the faces of a number of students, several of whom offer ideas furiously. Nadine offers examples from South Africa that she remembers from television accounts; Stephanie knows of torture in Central America and she relates a t.v. program which exposed the use of electrical torture devices there, imported from other countries. The students are making connections which may result in decisions they will make about their world and its peoples. The students are considering the shared information and taking a stand of their own. I find myself mediating and influencing their decisions by asking the questions: "Couldn't it [happen today]? Can you think of places where power is abused today?"

We move slowly through the reading of the chapters. I spend as much time explaining the Christmas story and responding to questions as I do reading the book, at first in order that they would "get the jokes," and later, because I know that this is an important story for them to know. Important, because stories from the Bible echo throughout our literature.

My role is not unlike that of the Greek pedagogue, the slave whose responsibility was to lead the way to show the child how to get to school and how to return, but it is leading, in the sense of accompanying and caring for the child in such a way as to provide direction for his or her life. What comes to mind for me is Max van Manen's (1991) description of the origin of the term:

> . . . a pedagogue is a man or woman who stands in a caring relation to children: in the idea of leading or guiding there is a "taking by the hand," in the sense of watchful encouragements. "Here, take my hand!" "Come, I shall show you the world. The way into a world, my world, and yours. I know something about being a child, because I have been there, where you are now. I was young once." (pp. 37-38)

By the time I finish reading aloud *The Best Christmas Pageant Ever* (1972) the students give it a high rating, higher than initially. Roey tells me he "liked the funny parts and the story about Jesus was really good, too."

I learn a tremendous amount about my students from reading this book: two go to church regularly and a few others had visited churches on a couple of occasions. By listening to their initial responses, I discover that they nearly missed out on a great deal of humor. I had a fine mentor in teaching who told me, "Sometimes you just have to **tell** the children certain things so that what you're discussing has a deeper meaning for them." In this case, it's a matter of sharing information about the Nativity story so the children can make the links for themselves. These references from Biblical stories resound throughout our western literature.

I feel there must be more I can do to help their understanding. In the school library I find a copy of *Christmas, the King James Version* (1984) with pictures by Jan Pienkowski. I think there may be problems with reading this book as the register of English would be too difficult. When language is beyond the grasp of the children's understanding, they deem the book to be 'boring'. However, we had created shadow puppets for folk tale plays earlier in the year that relied upon ornately cut black silhouettes placed against a dramatic background, so I knew the paper cuts and illuminated manuscript style of the book would draw my students' attention.

To my surprise their interest is high. We cannot get beyond the first paragraph without stopping.

"Oh, yeah, Herod," Paul and Judd chatter and smile, familiar with the ruler, they, members of the cognoscenti, share a cultural commonality. They get it this time.

"Where's Nazareth?" asks Emma, a front row fourth grader. A student fetches the atlas and we find it.

"That's near Lebanon," offers another student expert.

The hubbub begins about Lebanon and its problems and we are off the subject of the Nativity story again. Or are we? More television accounts are related until Danielle shyly turns to me and asks, "Ms. Sinclaire, why **are** they fighting over there?"

I hand the discussion back to the students and from the opinions presented, based on newspapers, television and parent opinions, the children share what they know.

We are talking once again of the misuse of power, the same misuse as in Herod's day.

The tittering begins. The term 'virgin' gets them. I explain, "The term 'virgin' at that time didn't mean a person who hadn't had sex, instead, it meant a young unmarried woman."

"Ooooohhh," they sigh in chorus, eyes wide, heads nodding, at hearing and understanding a taboo word in a different context with a different meaning.

The value of reading text with rich vocabulary is in the implicit message: words have origins; the meanings can change over time to be more general or more specific; etymologies are interesting. Words are interesting.

My students are taken back that there was no room at the inn. "Had they overbooked?" Theresa asks. "That's what happened to my parents last year in Hawaii."

I ask, "How do you think Mary and Joseph might have arranged ahead of time to stay at the inn?" Our discussion transports us back to a time before postage systems, travel agents, telephones, or fax.

About a month earlier my students had completed a lengthy pond water study in science. Some confusion resulted from the description of Mary, who, upon the visit of the Wise Men, learns their news sent from the angel of the Lord, and "pondered [these things] in her heart."

"What is 'ponder', Ms. Sinclaire? Is that something about ponds?" Perry inquires.

"No, good guess, though," I said. "To 'ponder' means to think about things," I respond.

"Well, what did she have to **ponder** about?" he asked insistently.

"Well, let's put it this way, Perry. You're at home and there's a knock at the door. You answer it and somebody says your mother is going to give birth to the Saviour of the world. How would your mom feel?"

Perry's eyes grew large and he smiles, "She'd have something to **think about**." I smile, too.

An arm waves furiously overhead, throttling the air. "Ms. Sinclaire, how **was** Jesus the Saviour of the world?" asks Adam, the curly headed boy at my feet.

I ponder this time, "How do I go about explaining pre-Christian religions without offending anyone?" Sacrifices are always a juicy topic, human or animal. I feel a delicate balance in discussion is vital in order that my students grow up to respect the beliefs and religions of all people. I do my best. Two students say they have been to church and know something about the rules Jesus laid down. Leah and Andrea share their expertise enthusiastically. Ideas from the students range from the Golden Rule through to the Ten Commandments. I can't recall all ten of them verbatim, but the students get the big ideas, with Leah helping out where I fall short. Rollie has a eureka experience with the commandments and belts out, "Those are just like our classroom rules, Ms. Sinclaire!"

More students chant in enthusiastic agreement, and much more readily than makes me comfortable, but I have to agree the commandments are rules to live by, anywhere.

Christmas is a short picture book, but this read-aloud and discussion is anything but short. We come to the last paragraph, "And the child grew, and waxed strong in spirit, filled with wisdom: and the grace of God was upon him." I am closing the book when I observe the many furrowed brows of the youngsters before me. Arms shoot up to question in every direction. The murmur grows into a roar. Judd and Roey yell out in unison, "Well, **then** what happened?"

"Yeah, what happened **next**?" Zach appeals.

I blurted out, "Don't you know?"

"No!" they answer.

Let me confess, I'm not a Bible authority. I've never taken instruction in Bible literature. These stories I heard, some I read. With my meagre knowledge, I tell my students that little is mentioned in the Bible about Jesus until much later in his adult years. I talk about how he began to preach and how he gathered disciples and that his following grew. Briefly, I mention that Jesus was brought to trial and was sentenced.

"What did they **do** to him?" the students demanded.

When I tell them of the crucifixion, some students want to know more about the details. The cross, the nails, I tell them all of it.

"But if He really was the Son of God, couldn't he get out of it?" Perry implores me, as though I had the power to reverse the action.

"Yeah, why not?" Melisa and Kacey join in.

Sacrifice, to explain to children the symbolic act of sacrifice! I think I fail here in my attempt to help my students understand the story. The crucifixion is a part of the story I haven't grasped yet myself.

For the next reading selection I turned to *The Selfish Giant* (1989) by Oscar Wilde. I always like to tell my students about authors in order that they see writers as real people who put pen to paper in the context of the period of time in which they lived. In sharing Oscar Wilde's life story, I tell them he was a married man with children who was nevertheless attracted to other men.

"He was a homosexual," shoots out Andrea, with a solemn expression on her face. I tell them how it was illegal to have such sexual relationships at that time, and that he had been sent to jail, only to contract tuberculosis, which ruined his health. The students consider his sentence and jail term unfair. Another misuse of power.

The Selfish Giant is the story of a giant who over-comes his selfishness to welcome children to his once forbidden garden and, in the end, is rewarded by an unusual, small child. This child returns to the garden, his hands bearing the prints of two nails, and upon his little feet the prints of two nails. While reading this part of the story aloud to my class, an enormous din of recog-nition rises from the students. They are insiders this time; they understand the significance of the symbols.

"Tell me about this story," I say at the end, inviting their ideas.

They all begin to chatter at once. "The little boy was just like Jesus."

"How?" I ask.

"His hands and feet had the nails in them," says Michelle.

Kacey offers, "That's not all, there's more. He helped the Giant to be generous. He was the Giant's Saviour."

"Yeah, the Giant wasn't a sinner any more," chimes in Aaron. "He's just like Jesus because—he took the Giant to Paradise."

The children formed insights about *The Selfish Giant* (1989) based on hearing *Christmas, the King James Version* (1989) and *The Best Christmas Pageant Ever* (1974) read-aloud and the discussions that took place from the readings. It was our talk together that helped the students to find deeper meanings of the broader, more universal issues from the stories. This leads me to consider several points. The first is that my role as a teacher as observer of children in the classroom is vital to student learning. When I observe students for their reactions, listen for their responses and ask them for their opinions, I discover not only what they do know but what they do not know. Through a sensitive way of talking and listening to children, I can help them to develop their understanding with information at a language level they can grasp. Through the readings and discussion I can help my students to stand amongst and become members of society who share associations with others. Furthermore, they can see that historical abuses can happen again if they are not recognized. My students enjoy being "in on the joke"; it enhances their motivation, self esteem and participation. In short, we must be talking about the same thing. Writers make assumptions about the body of information their readers know. The disadvantaged are those who do not know what that information is. When we share information we become members of a community.

Through the readings and discussion the children grow out of the world of childhood "(*educere:* to lead out of)" (van Manen, 1991, p. 38). "My world of adulthood becomes an invitation, a beckoning to the child (*educare:* to lead into)," writes van Manen (1991, p. 38). In this story I find myself alternately leading out of and leading into the children's understanding of themselves, others and the world. The classroom serves as a place where children learn to become someone by participating in their personal and moral growth, the process of which may serve to develop a conscience. They come to see themselves as part of the world within a historical, social and cultural perspective, their world, a larger 'home' on earth where they can participate and stand tall.

Standing Up for a Child

The next story is more narrowly focussed. It is a story in which I stand up for a child in order to help his mother understand her child's uniqueness. The mother seeks to live out her own unfulfilled ambitions through her children's futures, and in particular, through her son, Evan. In doing so, she doesn't see his qualities. It is difficult for this mother to allow enough distance from her son to see him as an independent being and to prevent confusing her own goals and desires with those of his. In standing alongside Evan, the mother and I confront that which is unique about him, and his future that lies beyond our grasp. In her understanding, she comes to accept her child and we both identify something about ourselves.

It is the last day of the school year, the day after the children receive their report cards and the teachers come back to have the year-end breakfast and "work in their rooms" until it's okay to leave. I like to work alone and I stay until 2:00 filing materials, tossing out files, and taking down displays so the room can be cleaned this summer. There are only three of our staff still in the school.

I hear a knock at the outer door—it's Beryl Harden, Evan's mom. She's almost six feet tall with leathery tanned skin. Beryl runs competitively and is both proud and embarrassed when she tells me that she came in third in the marathon this year. She has a direct way of talking and looking a person in the eye that intimidates some teachers but I admire those qualities in her.

"Hi, Beryl. Nice to see you." She must be here about Evan's report card. Quickly, I try to recall his grades but I am never good at details. There was improvement, I remember that.

"Yeah, I hoped I could catch you before you went," she says.

"Did you see Evan's report? Are you happy?" We both hover in the doorway of the school as she doesn't seem to want to enter.

"Yes, **I** was. And **so** was his father." She looks sheepish. "It's **Evan**. He's not too happy. He thought he should have done better."

Done better or received a better mark? "If I recall it's a report to be proud of. . . ." I am a little stunned by the response.

"Yeah, **we** thought so too. But he didn't think so." Beryl looks and sounds disappointed despite her words.

Beryl talks and I listen. Evan is comparing his marks in Language Arts to those of Roland, his best friend. They do everything together: soccer, guitar lessons, movies, read the same books. But when it comes to careful publishing, revising, editing and proof-reading, Rollie's work is exacting.

"You know I can't discuss Rollie's work with you, Beryl. But Evan needs to be careful when he checks his final copy. Also, he's a leftie so he has to put effort into making his handwriting legible."

"So it's sloppiness?" She pursues a hunch. "Does he rush? Does he want to be the first? Like me, he's very competitive." She looks proud at this statement.

"That's not my observation," I state. Beryl looks a little uncomfortable at this. "It's more a matter of making his piece so big it becomes unfocused. It's what I call the bed-to-bed story—every detail in it from the time you get up in the morning till the time you go to bed at night."

"Oh, yes. I remember typing a seven page story for him that he wrote in the third grade." She has the loving look only mothers could possess at this remembrance.

"Well, we move **away** from the bed-to-bed stories into tighter, focused writing and we select details that are relevant to the story. Of course, what's relevant to a child. . . ." My voice trails off and Beryl and I laugh, knowing the random thoughts of children.

I continue, "What I find with Evan is not racing to be first, it's adding more and more and more so that when it's time to revise and edit he's got too much. It's unwieldy and he can't get it finished."

"I **see**. . . ." Beryl trails off to her thoughts. "Should he be going to French immersion next year?" Mrs. Harden is asking me if they are making the right decision, and who ever knows about the fork in the road?

"Well, those are the same skills he'll need next year, whether he went to French immersion or an English speaking school. It's just more drill and practice where he's going," I say.

"We don't want him to do badly. I wonder. . . ."

"He's a good student, Beryl. He can keep working on these skills. He's made a lot of improvement this year. He's got all the ideas. He makes all the connections. And, he's a good reader." From her face I can see that my words are not assurance enough.

"He really enjoyed being in your class this year. The things you did. Your sense of humor. All the kids did."

Standing Side by Side with a Parent

"Thanks." I hesitate for a moment but I have to ask, "Could some of his unhappiness about this grade be due to the fact that his sister did so well at school, and that he compares himself to her grades?" Beryl looks a little uncomfortable, but she doesn't deny it. We are talking candidly, and she understands that what I am asking is in Evan's best interests.

"Could be? Yeah." There is a long pause and she opens up a little more. "Well, actually, **her** grades were different this time too. They were A's, B's and C's, well C pluses, too, of course. But they **weren't** all A's. . . . This is the first time that. . . . Could that **be**?" Beryl looks at me for guidance.

"Well, she's a teen now. It's possible that she's identifying her interests and committing herself to those instead of trying to succeed in everything." I want to assure Beryl. She has seen a rent form in the fabric she has woven. Perhaps these children won't continue to measure up to their early promise and to her hopes. I tell her about myself, "When I was a teenager my report was all A's in English Literature, French and Art but C's and even C–'s in Math and Science. I even failed P.E. and Home Ec."

"Well, **I** was okay in P.E. But the rest. . . ." She looks off in the distance. "I never had the good marks these kids have." Is this a case of Beryl's own dreams being vicariously realized through these children? A chance for her own mistakes to be eradicated?

"You know, Beryl, life gives us all many chances at the brass ring."

"I know. I know. But still." Her voice is heavy with regret. I know too. I am a high school drop out who went to university at thirty. The pauses in our conversation are filled with reflection on what has been said and on what remains unsaid.

"Beryl, they're both kids. They have good work habits. I wouldn't worry about either of them."

"Well, we're sending the girl to private school next year." She sighs and stands a little taller, sending a mixed message of hope, resignation and fear. "We're hoping it'll give her a good foundation. French Immersion didn't work out for her."

"It's not for everybody."

"That's why we were so afraid . . . , no, **concerned**, about whether we were making the best decision for Evan."

"It's hard to know, isn't it?" I sympathize.

"Yeah."

Getting Closer to Understanding

I hesitate before sharing my thoughts with her. "The hardest, I think, is learning to live with our own . . .

mediocrity . . . and **mediocrity** isn't the best word—it's too strong."

We volley synonyms, smiling at each other.

"Shortcomings," she tries out.

"Abilities. . . ."

"Imperfections. . . ."

"Inadequacies. . . ."

"Well, we **know** what we mean," she says and laughs.

"We're talking about the same thing."

"Thanks," she says. "I appreciate it." We both feel a gratitude for the depths of what we have shared. The conversation evolved from one simple beginning and gained in its profundity.

We nod and smile as our eyes connect. Beryl isn't a hugger, but we have embraced the problem. It is ourselves. We are silent in the gaze we hold. This is a "fulfilled silence" where "the truth, not only of the insight that has been acquired, but the truth of life, the state of being in truth that has been achieved in the conversation, continues to make itself felt, indeed becomes deeper, in the course of this silence." (Bollnow, 1982, p. 46) The truths we have arrived at resonate more profoundly than the mere topic of a report card or the expectations for a child, but echo deeper from Beryl's unfulfilled expectations for herself and mine as well. For Beryl and I, both parent and teacher, must have: "a sense of the meaning of being human, a sense of hope for the personal becoming of the child, and finally, an untiring sense of patience to hold the expectations and other requirements of the adult in check." (Bollnow, 1989, p. 11)

Beryl must see the differences between her children and herself so that she can strengthen her children. To do that, Beryl must take into consideration Evan's interests and unique abilities, particularly those that do not encompass her own. In recognizing her own intent, she begins to stand alongside Evan, but separate and apart in order that he develop his self-sufficiency.

Helping a Child Stand Up for Herself

In the final story of this chapter, my reading and personal telling of pet stories in the classroom release further telling of pet stories by the children—stories of loss of pets and loss of trust in parents, disappointment, disillusionment and rage. Sylvana, my most taciturn student shares hers, and the effect of the story goes further than I expect. As a result, I receive a visit from her mother, who also has a pet story to tell that has gone unheard for many years. I had never considered the degree of effect of my honesty in the classroom before this day. My telling represents a model for students to take a stand, and that stand, in this particular case creates an occasion for honesty and understanding within a home. I see my student, Sylvana, in a different light after she tells her story; her voice is released for the rest of our year together.

It began the morning I brought in *Every Living Thing* (1985) by Cynthia Rylant and read "A Pet", the story about Emma, a little girl who "begged so hard for a Christmas pet that her parents finally relented and gave her the next best thing: a goldfish." (p.26) The goldfish was "used," both old and blind. Emma's parents, both lawyers, argued that money could buy better things than flea collars; that she had been unnecessarily influenced by too many Walt Disney movies; and that she should spend time with her viola, not with an animal. The story is delicately, if not tragically told, with the slow but inevitable death of the pet and its burial. My students are intense with their quiet listening. There is a resonance in pet stories that end in loss.

A slight movement alters the stillness as the students' attention unfurls. There is the shuffling of feet, as a few students shake loose from the mood.

I tell my own first pet story, the one I told the night before as a student in my Children's Literature course. Then I was stirred by emotion as I recalled the events, but it didn't show. This morning, as I unravel the threads to the past, I've spiralled deeper into the midst of my feelings of thirty-odd years ago. I'm unaware of the tears that well, and then gush down my cheeks in front of the children, as I tell my story. I hear, "Look, teacher's crying," followed by, "Shhh, I want to hear!"

I don't lose my momentum for I am compelled to tell. "We really couldn't afford to have another pet . . . I know that now, but I didn't understand it at the time." Telling is understanding at a deeper level, rearranging, re-engaging in the story to select the vital parts. I tell of the grey kitten I found surrounded by a mob of taunting children who poured fence paint on him.

"He tried to wipe the paint out of his eyes, but all those kids did was laugh. I was so angry I burst through and grabbed him. They tried to pull him away from me, but I pushed through them, and I ran all the way home with the kitten in my arms, smearing paint all over my clothes. My parents, they weren't mean. After all, my brother had one cat and they felt that was more than enough. But I knew they wouldn't refuse me taking care of the kitten until it was healthy and safe."

My students are leaning forward, many with their hands cupping their chins. They're wearing the warm smiles of expectancy that says everything will turn out okay.

"My mom gave me a bunch of old, soft towels to mop off as much paint as I could, and even my dad, who was determined not to have 'another mangy creature in the house', hovered behind, making suggestions."

"'You have to cut off those clumps of paint before he tries licking himself. It is a 'he' isn't it? God, imagine, more kittens. Sheeesh! Perish the thought! Here, I'll get the scissors'."

"Fluffy, that's what I named him, although he wasn't fluffy at the time and he never would be, sat very still and looked up into our faces. I knew my parents were sold on keeping him, at least I hoped they would be."

"Later, when his hair grew back, they gave in to my pleas with harsh warnings, 'You keep him—then you're responsible for his care and for his clean up. Don't expect us to pay for any vet visits. You'll have to pay for that fancy cat food out of your chore money. And if he gets sick on the rug, you clean it up or out he goes.'"

"'Yes, mom. Okay, dad.' I was never happier. I had a pet of my own."

"That summer I painted fences, mowed lawns, and weeded gardens for all the neighbours. Oh, and I walked pets. I earned enough to keep Fluffy in cat food for a long time. But I never earned enough for the vet shots. And then Fluffy got sick."

"'Don't worry, he'll get over it, all cats get sick. He'll eat some grass and he'll be fine. Cats are smart. They know how to take care of themselves,' my dad said."

"But Fluffy didn't get better. Only worse."

Some of my students are covering their eyes now. The faces I can see are long. I tell of his burial under the lilac bush, my stiff little kitten wrapped in old gift wrap, purple tissue paper, a wrinkled satin ribbon tied around the shoe box.

Many students are crying now. Not so much for my story, but for all the pets they've loved and lost. No one asks, "Couldn't they do something?" and no one says,

"Your parents were mean." There is an acceptance: that's the way it was.

Deanna and Bethany leave the room wiping their eyes. Tim hides his face, wiping his nose on a sleeve.

Mark is the first to speak and he's angry. "That's just what Roger did. I had a nice German Shepherd puppy and Roger wouldn't pay for shots and he got distemper. We had to put him down because he got dangerous and tried to bite kids. Mark's voice is full of rage as he blurts out, "I loved that dog!" His mouth turns to a wistful smile for the memories he holds. "He used to race alongside my bicycle down Fleming Avenue all the way to the river."

Many dog and cat and bird stories are told. Stories of having to move and the pet which was left behind with a neighbour. Some get loved and some neglected. Stories of not being asked or told about a pet dropped off at the S.P.C.A. Just "He's lost." Later the truth slips out by accident. The pets differ as do the circumstances, but the the longing is the same.

Sylvana is a new student this year, a repeater. She is a great, glum, dark girl whose black eyes sulk behind a greasy fringe of bangs. She is shadowy and festering most of the time—silent, I feel, with an anger brooding. She has not said one word in class this year and now it is November. She doesn't answer in class and offers grunts "yeah" or "no" when I sit next to her to talk about her work. I suspect that Sylvana's is a "defiant silence" that echoes a conflict at home, which may have brought about her refusal to communicate at all. She has been unable or unwilling to expose herself by speaking openly in class. Perhaps silence is Sylvana's self-protection. (Bollnow, 1982, pp. 42-3)

But this morning she doesn't wait to put her hand up to share. Instead, she stares straight ahead and begins loudly with a voice driven by anger, "My uncle. He did that. Backed right over my dog in the driveway with his truck. He never even said 'I'm sorry.' Never said anything. Just left my dog there on the road. He hates dogs. I **hate** my uncle."

We are shocked to hear her voice but we are more shocked by the force of her story and the brutality of the act. Time passes and a few more stories are told but we are still in the grip of Sylvana's.

"Well, enough?" I ask softly, knowing that this is one of the most difficult transitions we can make into class "work." "Shall we write these?"

"No, not just yet. . . ." a few students say, the rest agree. It's too soon, we're unsettled. Perhaps, tomorrow. Tomorrow, we'll be ready to write.

A week later Sylvana's mother comes in to see me to talk about her "little girl." Mrs. Constantino is in her late thirties, a short woman, blanketed in excess weight.

She begins, "We felt it was best to have her repeat. Her last year's teacher said she needed to work on her skills. I took her advice. It was a new neighbourhood. I wasn't sure. . . ."

I listen and see the anguish on this mother's face. She is troubled about her decision and its effect on Sylvana, so much taller than the rest in size, but so short in confidence.

She continues, "I don't know what you've done. She **likes** it here. She likes **you**. She likes the class."

"Oh," I say, mouth agape. "I didn't know. . . ."

Mrs. Constantino doesn't stop to notice my surprise. Instead, she blurts out, "Sylvana told me she talked about her dog in class. You know, she's never talked about that dog at home. We just let it pass. We thought she got over it. But I guess. . . ." She falters and begins to sob. Her massive chest heaves up and down and she hides her eyes with a plump fist. Then she wails, "We had her uncle over that night and we all . . . talked." She half laughs, "And we cried a bit, too. Her uncle, you know, he didn't know she saw. He thought we'd just get her another dog. He doesn't like dogs but he always felt so bad about what happened. He just couldn't say."

I put my hand on Mrs. Constantino's wrist and rub her hand. She cries again, this time a soft far-away cry from a place inside her from long ago. I sit alongside her in silence, not intervening, allowing her the time to be in touch with her feelings and thoughts, to breathe and speak when she is ready.

"I had a little dog, too, you know . . . when I was about Sylvana's age. Susie, that was her name. My mother didn't like that dog. She was always underfoot and tracking in mud. Susie got sick and my dad took her out and shot her. I **loved** that little dog. And nobody asked me. He just **did** it."

Mrs. Constantino and I sit side by side, two grown women, heaving and sobbing. We cry for our pets lost long ago and for Sylvana's more recent loss. We mourn for the permission never requested of us as children to take away the things we love most. We cry for all the apologies not forthcoming. We weep for our own voices mute all these years. We connect with our own anger and hurt entombed within us long ago, and we release it. After a time we have only sniffles left. We remain silent in a "wordless agreement" in which we understand each other's innermost thoughts and no words are necessary. (Bollnow, 1982, p. 44)

Mrs. Constantino chokes, "Thank you for listening," and leaves.

I am stunned by the ripple effect of reading a pet story and telling my own in class. Sylvana has found her voice, and with it she has taken a stand in the world.

She attends to her woundedness, her pain, her anguish, to her self that she has ignored and denied. In doing so, she honours her needs, in hope that they may heal. It prompts the voice of her mother to express the pain that she has denied so many years.

Sylvana is learning to simply listen and be present to herself and others. She must "remember as she seeks her own voice, that she will emerge only when she speaks from her own true nature and experience, only when she expresses what she cares most dearly about, and [that which] is her own unique and individual truth." (Duerk, J. pp. 64-6) Her task is to know herself and let her personal truth emerge.

I step aside from the story to reflect on Max van Manen's words (1991):

> Leading means going first, and in going first you can trust me, for I have tested the ice. I have lived. I now know something of the rewards as well as the trappings of growing towards adulthood and making a world for yourself. Although my going first is no guarantee of success for you (because the world is not without risks and dangers), in the pedagogical relationship there is a more fundamental guarantee: No matter what, I am here. And you can count on me. (p. 38)

It seems that I am "leading" in the classroom even when I am unaware of it. The parts of my life that I openly share with my students come from my own maturation after confronting my own suffering; this may help the children understand their sorrows. (Bollnow, 1989, pp. 60-61) My own experience and security with a situation may be a model for them to emulate, something to alleviate their sadness. When teachers tell their own stories passionately to their students, it frees their students to release the longings they hold within. As a result of my storytelling, Sylvana tells her story in class and at home, which transforms a family secret into an honest conversation between father, mother, uncle and child. The intimacy of 'home' is felt again in Sylvana's home, as a result of the telling in class. When the teacher 'leads' and provides the assurance that children will be heard, the capacity to lead is encouraged in children.

Although unfortunate, these losses lead us to a greater maturity; the opportunity to discuss them with others leads to a more authentic existence. "The task of the adult lies in comforting and being available in the face of such threats," Bollnow reminds us. (1989, p. 10) The child's world is expanded by the teacher's knowledge of the world the child is entering and by the teacher's attunement to the child. The teacher leads and follows the child over a bridge of learning and experiences which prepare the child for an understanding of self, others and finding a home in the world. At times, the stance of the adult, whether parent or child is one of standing side by side with the child until he or she can stand alone and, subsequently, like Sylvana, begin to lead others in their search for home.

6

Commemoration and Celebration

I conclude this book with stories in which I highlight the importance of commemorating and celebrating the home we have made for ourselves in the classroom and the understandings we have created beyond it, in our home in the world.

"Awards!? Not awards? I have to write out those certificates after I've slaved away for days on report cards? Haven't I said it **all** already?" I think to myself when the topic of the year-end certificates is brought up at the staff meeting. My colleague and I discuss it afterwards.

"Aren't they ridiculous? They don't mean anything to the kids. They just throw them out."

"It's just more empty public relations for the school. What a waste of time and money," my colleague adds.

"Okay, I'll just **do** it!" I resign myself to the task, as I reluctantly grab a handful of the heavy bond embossed certificates from the cupboard. I didn't understand then the function of ceremonies and celebrations in school life as "indispensable dimensions of human living without which life cannot be complete. (Bollnow, 1989, p. 66) I would come to recognize ceremonies and celebrations as a necessary part of education with a special purpose in schools. (Bollnow, 1989, p. 66)

"Oh, goodee! We're doing the awards today!" I hear Aaron announce as he comes in to read the morning schedule.

"Oh, I love awards!" Andrea shouts.

"You mean certificates, don't you, Ms. Sinclaire?" Paul asks.

"Yes, you're right, Paul," I say.

"Can we do them now?" Brittany wheedles, "Ple . . . e . . ease?"

"After recess . . . after our silent reading time," I say firmly.

"O-kay," the students chime in with a certain amount of disappointment.

Quiet fills the room during our reading until the appointed moment—11:05. That's when silent reading is officially over.

"Awards, Ms. Sinclaire."

Michelle never forgets. Those who prefer to sit at their desks to read join us quickly at the carpet. There is no hesitation. I place the stack of certificates on my lap as I sit on the tiny yellow chair.

The students and I have come to experience the deeper significance in our being together in the classroom over the last year, and, for some students, two years. This is the only occasion in the school year in which I take the time to remind all the students in detail of the qualities each and every child possesses and has brought to the classroom. It is only in the "respectful observance of ceremony" that we can experience the "fullness" of our growth. (Bollnow, 1989, p. 67) This ceremony marks a "decisive point or passage into a new phase of life" for each child—to leave behind the assurance of the familiar, to acknowledge his or her own growth, maturity, and, most importantly, to step into a new exchange between students, and students and teacher next September. (Bollnow, 1989, p. 68) We experience the significance of this year end award ceremony by taking part in the mood. (Bollnow, 1989, p. 68)

I look at the children's faces to gauge the mood. There is a hush, not an enthusiastic eagerness, but an expectancy in the air. "What will be said about me? What have I done that will receive honourable mention?" their faces seem to ask. I wonder if I have chosen what they deem to be true and important about themselves. There is a solemnity here. I am reminded of the magnitude of solemnity in ceremonies by Bollnow's (1989) words:

> Solemnity is the mood of ceremony in which authority finds itself. Here one encounters the fuller and deeper significance of life. That is why ceremonies are, above all, memorial ceremonies. One is to remember a past event, something historical, or the birth of a significant person. Through the ceremony the person becomes directly present to us, as is possible only in thoughtful reflection. This event is not just grasped in a theoretic sense; rather, it is immediately present to us in its signifying power. The distinguishing characteristic is that one steps out of the world of everyday life and into the solemn world of the ceremonial mood. (p. 67)

As I do a quick talk about the certificates being different from report cards, I am not entirely clear about the difference myself. "These are different from report cards because they may refer to something that isn't a subject, like math. They refer to a talent you have or a special skill. Or maybe how you've made the class a better place to be this year."

The students listen more intently than normally. Their faces are serious and their eyes are on me—and the certificates. They seem to understand the purpose of certificates better than I do and they do not interrupt to say, "Yeah, we know all that" as they might about other things. This is a ceremony and they are conducting themselves accordingly. Yet, I must guide them to recognize this occasion as a ceremony in order to prepare them inwardly to accept what has been meaningful about our time together, and afterwards, to bring it to a conclusion.

I begin to read off the inscriptions when Aaron interrupts, "Ms. Sinclaire, instead of giving the name first, could you read out the description?"

"Yeah, yeah," Perry joins in, "And then we could guess who it is."

"That would be better," Paul says.

"More fun," Stephanie says, her eyes lighting up as she jostles Michelle with her elbow, pointing out the possibilities.

What is an exhausting formality for me has become a guessing game for my students. At the end of the year after reports I feel emptied of words. Now they will discover the emptiness of the inscriptions. They could probably apply to anybody in the class. I have struggled to find the words that match the child. I loathe empty rituals. Oh well, here goes. . . .

I begin, "This one goes to a person for his leadership ability. . . ."

I don't get the chance to finish the part about "organizing hat days" when the students are half-whispering, half-shouting, "It's Perry!" Perry is beaming.

"And it goes to Perry!" I finish off game show style, hiding the sound of relief in my voice that it is, indeed, Perry.

I hold up the next award, blocking the name from sight, "And for his public relations skills that earn him so many friends. . . ."

"Allan! It's Allan. It's gotta be Allan!" And it is Allan. But how do they know? .

"For her ability to speak out . . ." I announce, but already they're shouting, chanting, "Stephanie! Stephanie! Stephanie!"

". . . for just causes," I finish.

They drone on in agreement, "Stephanie, Stephanie, Stephanie."

There is no doubt—it's Stephanie. She knows it too. Her face beams a tomato shade while all her orthodontistry gleams in the sun pouring in the window. She reads the certificate to herself, holding it out in front of her, and presses it to her chest as carefully as a mother holds a newborn.

With their spontaneous guessing, my students are turning the solemnity of ceremony into a festive celebration. Through their participation they can submerge themselves in this mood which is so different from everyday life. The bond between the students is affirmed; Stephanie is recognized for her individual qualities, not only by me, but by her peers. In modern festive celebration, "The human being moves out of the isolation of his or her everyday existence into a situation of great bliss and finds himself or herself accepted into a new communion." (Bollnow, 1989, p. 70) It is not just that the experience of the communion brings Stephanie happiness; it is, on the contrary, the enhanced mood brought on by the festivity of guessing that allows her to experience this communion.

"And this one goes to a fellow for his practical problem-solving ideas," I say.

"It's Evan! Yep, Evan," several boys cheer. I look

towards Evan as the eagerness disappears from his face only to be replaced with disappointment. He had expected something else. This is not the way he sees himself. Only 'Academic Excellence' will do, I suppose, and he doesn't qualify. Besides, I purposely did not write certificates that pointed to academic merit. Two years ago, in third grade, academic awards were given for scholarship, citizenship and sports. Evan had thought himself to be the scholar and so had his parents. They roared into the principal's office after storming the phones in protest. The teacher stood firm. The principal backed her up. The award went to another student. But Evan's mother wants to see her hopes realized in her son. Evan's sister was a scholar. Not Evan. He works hard, but he's not a scholar. And now his face contorts. He smiles as he receives his certificate but it's a mask to conceal his disappointment and anger.

His friends whisper to him, "Oh, neat. I wish she'd said that about me."

"Yeah, that's **good**, Ev." Evan looks at them quizzically and softens.

"For her kindness and her tact . . ." I hesitate. This one is harder to figure out for there are four or five girls who could be singularly identified this way.

"Melisa."

"Tara."

"Leah."

"Michelle."

"Bianca" the crowd offers. All are mentioned by the students and I am a little embarrassed, wondering how the rightful owner will feel and how the runners-up will handle this. Nothing to worry about.

The children buoy up the spirits of all concerned when I announce, "And it's Tara!"

"Well, it **could have been** Leah."

"Or Melisa."

"Michelle, too," they add.

I read a similar certificate and I hear Kacey say, "That's **gotta** be Melisa this time."

They recognize the subtle differences in the description of Melisa's qualities and those of Leah. Melisa reads her certificate silently, mouthing the words, and smiles as she identifies herself with those qualities. As teacher, mentor, friend, I am the person endowed with authority to identify for each child, his or her gifts. I choose the moments and attribute significance to them. I see from her smile, Melisa does, too.

"This certificate is given to a fellow here for his sweet smile. . . ."

The students smile and nod, deciding at once, "It's Josh." Josh struggled and gave up early this year. Each morning he would arrive late, and only at his father's insistence. He would heave himself listlessly into his seat and his body would sink into a mass of ripples. His eyes would glaze over and he would drift into a daydream.

"Huh, what?" he'd say as I gave him instructions on my knees at his side. "I can't find it. I left it at home. What? I don't get it," he'd say wistfully. Josh **didn't** get it, not all year, not even on one day. It was a struggle for me to write a certificate for this boy. I am wary about how he will receive his comment. Will the others mock him? Will he be ashamed that this is the quality I see in him? I half expect a sarcastic reply from some students but none is ventured. Most students want their unique qualities to be identified. Josh would just like to be the same. He shares in the joy of the occasion because he has the a certificate in his hands too. All the students are content.

More awards. Some are so easy to write and give. "For his storytelling ability. . . ."

"Aaron! Aaron!" the crowd cheers. Aaron is the catalyst. He gets each morning going with his tales of frog-catching and admissions of petty crimes that open the door to real discussion about things important to the kids.

"For her sense of fun. . . ." I'm smiling thinking of all of Kacey's stories about boyfriends, going steady, kissing and giving rings. Even though I know of Kacey's family troubles, this is what I will remember most about her.

"Kacey," the class answers. Everyone knows.

We end. Every student is proudly holding a Riverside Elementary certificate. We have experienced a deeper communion amongst ourselves which ensued in the festive celebration through guessing. In this experience we come closer to one another, we feel joined together.

At once, Stephanie speaks out, "What about you, Ms. Sinclaire? You didn't get a certificate!"

Brittany offers, "Yeah, can we make you one? Me and Bianca?"

A cluster of kids tightens about me, "Yeah, instead of doing that other thing?"

They refer to a nearly complete project of 'wishes' for their own futures. They are enjoying the project, but this moment of certificates is more immediate. As their teacher, I am without commemoration. And the students are qualified to recognize my abilities.

"Okay, here's the forms . . . but write a rough draft first. Okay?" Always I am the teacher, pointing to the process of writing and revision and concerned about the misuse of paper. Stephanie and Michelle grab dictionaries and the official award forms, complete with curlicues and insignia.

Nadine tells me she doesn't need a form, "Lily and me are going to make our own."

Lily leaves giggling and I think I'll have to accept a

little ridicule in these awards the children make for me. Perhaps this teasing will serve to ease our year-end parting. (Bollnow, 1989, p. 65) The chatter is intense, but soft, so as to keep secret their declarations. As I circulate around the room, their shoulders bend in such a way as to shield their works from the gaze of onlookers. Their heads are angled, their tongues out, they are intense in their execution of their ideas.

"Don't look, Ms. Sinclaire! It's got to be a surprise," Brittany scolds.

"She didn't see, did she?" Bianca asks, her voice worried that the ceremony might be spoiled for me.

A little while later, the children cluster around me. Some hold their certificates behind their backs, shielding their surprise which is to be held out till the last minute. Stephanie and Michelle are fifth graders, the older girls, so they get to go first by some unwritten law in the classroom. They are interested only in their certificates and my reactions to them. They look both proud and anxious as they await my reaction. I read each one aloud,

> This certificate is awarded to
> Ms. Sinclaire
> For her abilities to have
> neat clothes, good sence
> of humor and weird hair
> all at the same time.

It is a personal exchange. Michelle's inscription is similar but she adds "kindness" to the list of qualities. We laugh and smile at each other and I give thanks.

Then they are off with, "We gotta finish our wish lists now."

The younger girls encircle me now. They call themselves 'The Divas' for a club they have formed. Brittany chews on her waist length hair while Bianca drops her thick lashes down to shade her eyes from view. Lily is not shy, she looks straight at me, her eyes large, her mouth wide in a tight smile, as she plunges her arm forward to thrust a small macabre picture into my hands. Blood drips from a long manicured hand, clutching at life from the sea. It says, "SO LONG (For the Summer Maybe!)"

A devil rises from the end of a pitchfork threatening a possible return. "This is you," she points to the hand desperately clutching at life; "This is me," she says, indicating the devil. Lily has told me I'd better save a place for her in my class next year—"or else!"

"There's something on the back," she says shyly. I turn it over and begin to read out loud.

Lily stops me with, "No, that's private. Just **you** get to read it." She tilts her head on one side and twirls her hair as her bravado disappears. I read it to myself,

> you were
> A good Teacher!
> from
> ?
> Lillian Georgina
> Bag ley

Lillian, forever the teaser, gave me several horrifying pictures of myself this year, one for Valentine's Day with swelling cleavage and blood-shot eyeballs, my hair awry. At first I didn't know what to think. So, she even makes fun of **her** name.

Bianca, Brittany and Amber have designed their awards too. Amber's is covered with smiling sun symbols wearing eye shades. It reads,

Award Award Award!!
This award is presented to . . .
Ms. Sinclaire
For: Being kind and having a great sence of humor!!
sincerly, Amber
Date: June 25

Bianca's is simply illustrated and to the point. It says,

For Ms. Sinclaire
Coments Thank you for your
good listening, sense of
humor and strong speaking
voice.
From: Bianca
06-25

Brittany's certificate has elaborate detailed drawings that trail from a header that consists of my first name in huge block print. What a thrill the children have in using my first name, for that is treading into dangerous and forbidden territory for the students in this school. They savour it, rolling it deliciously around over their tongues—"Carollyne." As they try it out in front of me, they act as if they had run over, pinched a friend, and run away again to see if they would get chased and caught.

Brittany and Bianca look for my reaction to the certificate. It is decorated with flourish: children slide down the letters on the certificate, balance precariously from capital Ls and sun themselves from the ellipsis that trails from 'Carollyne' while I hover in miniature form in the back tearing at my hair. It reads:

CAROLLYNE . . .
To Carollyne Sinclaire
For Your All Around Achivment
Brittany

The seventh graders received their awards and certificates in the gym the previous day at an all-school
assembly. The most coveted award, 'All-Around
Achievement', goes to a combination of qualities: out-
standing citizen, academic scholar and athlete.
Certainly, I am no athlete. Do the children hint at something unspoken in our relationship with their vague
descriptions of my characteristics: "good sence of humor
and weird hair all at the same time," "kindness" and
"all-around achivment?" Perhaps words do not express
Brittany's feelings at this time. Or perhaps she's just
trying the words on for size.

The awards are in my hands and 'thank you' alone
does not seem enough. A hug will have to do. The students dart away to finish some things and start others.
Most of these children I've known for two years. We know
each other well.

The awards speak louder than the report cards.
Report cards are limited to 'can-dos' in the realm of aca-
demic-intellectual, social-emotional and social responsibility categories, all the jargon of the time. Our ceremony, with its certificates and spontaneous
participation, celebrates us as human beings who know
and care about each other. We recognize our feeling of
belonging together through our ceremony turned celebration of which we are not aware of in the normal run of
the school year. We are part of a community in the deep-
est sense, people who are at home with each other. We
commemorate our special qualities that we value in each
other. I read my awards now, as the children did earlier,

and press them closer to my heart. They are all I take home from the classroom on the last day of the school year.

Commemorating a Life Story

The next story also begins with the solemn mood and formal speech of ceremony. Yet, within the solemn mood of this story there arises the opportunity for festive celebration when Mr. Koyama, a senior citizen and my former beginner English student in Japan, visits me in Canada to tell me his life story. He has obviously pre-pared and rehearsed the speech in advance. The manner in which he tells his story is solemn and formal, inter-rupted by cathartic emotion, for he recalls the death of his friends and comrades with whom he was interned for six years in a Russian prisoner of war camp in Tashkent while he was able to survive. The past is immediately present for him during his commemorative speech to me.

"Do you want to hear my life story?" Mr. Koyama asks me, his head tilted graciously on one side. His ques-tion has the rehearsed tone that gives away his search for the 'right word in English' and plenty of practice beforehand with written pages.

Mr. Koyama was my English student in Sapporo, Japan, six years ago where I taught a 'Silver Club' class for senior citizens sponsored by a large newspaper com-pany. He and his wife were now part of a tour group staying at the Hotel Vancouver. Months before his trip, he wrote to request a visit with me in September. In my class abroad, he was late to join the tight-knit little group composed of retired professional gentlemen and the wives of bankers, doctors and businessmen. They came to learn English for travel, for diversion, for prestige, and most important, for company. Mr. Koyama was not easily accepted by the group, not so much for his late arrival, but for his unsuitable social outbursts. At lunch he would get drunk and make lewd remarks that the other members could not subdue.

Mr. Koyama clears his throat. "Okay. Then I begin. I was a student in Tokyo—Waseda University. Waseda, you know?" I nod, impressed with his credentials for acceptance into one of Japan's finest universities. He had never struck me as having such a beginning.

"Very happy, good life." He leans back and narrows his eœyes to lines as though to better focus his memory on the past. "I went to enjoy the army," he tells me. As an English teacher in Japan I came to learn that in Japanese-English to "enjoy" is used to mean "to participate in."

His chest swells a little and he sits erect. "I was a military officer in charge of **m-a-n-y** men." He lengthens the word 'many' and I have visions of his troops standing before him at attention.

"They sent us to Sakhalin. Do you know?"

"Yes, the Sakhalin Islands, north of Japan."

"Sakhalin is Japan," he states firmly. "Then invasion of Manchu, you know Manchu?"

"Yes, Manchuria."

"There we were taken prisoner and sent to **U**. . . . **S**. . . . **S**. . . . **R**." Mr. Koyama emphasizes each letter. "Tashkent. They sent us to Tashkent. Five years—forced labour. Do you know forced labour?" he insists. His eyes are intense.

"Yes," I say, shrinking back, thinking, "I know **of** forced labour but I do not truly know forced labour."

"Many of my friends died. Dear friends." Mr. Koyama hesitates a long time before he says, "I think of them for many years and I cry. Now, still, I think of them and I cry."

My eyes fill with tears, for I have heard my father echo Mr. Koyama's words about his friends who died in Japanese prisoner of war camps. On the night before I flew to Japan for my teaching assignment in 1984, my father sat me down at the kitchen table, doing little to hold back the anger in his voice, and repeated the P.O.W. stories with more vivid details than I'd heard before: accounts of beatings, cruelty and starvation. I had heard of forced labour. But in Canada, during the recession, I was without a teaching job. Japan offered me what I wanted. To my father, in some way, I was a traitor.

Mr. Koyama moves close to me, his eyes burning with rage. "I cry but **I don't hate**," his voice seething, as he emphasizes the last three words. He repeats again, "**I don't hate**," this time louder. His head falls to one side and his voice mocks, ". . . because . . . I am . . . Japanese . . . and we do not express that emotion." Each syllable bursts forth from clenched teeth. He stiffens and returns to himself and repeats this time in neutral tones, "I do not hate."

We both sit silent, breathing deeply, regaining our equilibrium. He begins again, "Now I am happier. But always I think of my friends who died . . . and I, . . . I live."

He looks at me. "Five years of forced labour. Do you know forced labour?" he implores. He shakes his head slowly and he recounts wearily, "Very hard. The war is over and I return to Hokkaido. I have nothing. I start again. But I am old."

Mr. Koyama leans forward and tilts his head a little, as if to ask understanding. He says, "I miss my chance."

In Japan there are career steps that begin to weed the successful early in life. Performance in junior high school determines the choice of senior high, which, in turn, is the factor that selects the candidates for the prestigious university. Graduation from such a university ensures the good job, the good life, with benefits that far exceed salary, housing and retirement.

"I miss my chance. I too old. But I try anyway. Do you know Fujitsu?" Mr. Koyama looks for a reaction in me. His arms stretch wide as he says, "World's largest computer company—**v-e-ry** big. Do you know?"

I regret that I do not know. For to know the size of Fujitsu is to know that Mr. Koyama is part of the grandeur of that company. "I.B.M. and Macintosh I know. Maybe soon I'll know Fujitsu."

He ignores my compliment and returns to his story. "I too late. I miss my chance." With these words the furrows deepen on his face and his body sags a bit. His voice is neutral as he says, "I have good life. Wife, family. Still, I cry, you know?" He looks at me for understanding and blurts out, "Five years! Forced labour. . . ." His voice trails off in regret, "So many friends dead. . . ."

Koyama-san looks at me directly and switches into a less rehearsed form of speech. "I want you know. All time I want tell you in Sapporo but I not English."

We look at each other for what seems a long time.

"I happy man now." "Happy," he smiles and beats his chest with one fist and reaches over to his gift for me, hibiscus carved in wood. "Happy," he repeats, "woodcarver, very good." "Ichiban woodcarver," he laughs and points to his wife who has remained seated, listening in silence to his story. "Family, wife, happy." "Silver Club, start happy. Carol-san, number one teacher!" Mr. Koyama is giving me, his former teacher the two thumbs up. He laughs and grins and his wife joins him, waving the two thumbs up sign, giving the cheer in Japanese.

The laughter subsides and he hangs his head for a moment. Then he looks deeply into my eyes and says,

"You come Sapporo. You teach us English. You make us laugh. We young again. You come back." Mr. Koyama found a 'home' for his restless soul with this group; he wanted me to return home to be with all its members.

Celebrating a New Life

We did laugh a lot as a class. The Silver Club was my second assignment, my first adults after a series of English classes with preschoolers. Eager to learn commands in Japanese to get the attention of the toddlers, I quickly picked up the language I heard my Japanese team teaching partner use. I was floundering with all the assignments, and in my exhaustion, I had been cutting my Japanese lessons. I was not aware that I was learning Japanese baby talk!

Armed with my flashcards, textbook and visual aids, I entered my first Silver Club class, with an air of confidence from a few Japanese commands. After introductions, we got to the review part where I held up flashcards. I thought I'd sprinkle in my first Japanese command, "Kore nan-da?" (What's this?") The men gasped, turned red, and attempted to hold back their laughter. The women covered their mouths with a hand and giggled. Once they had made eye contact with another Silver Club member, there was no holding the laughter back. My intonation and pitch resembled that of the Japanese instructor, I thought. I repeated the same instruction and they roared. Mr. Yamamoto, a very tall and sedate gentleman, took off his glasses and wiped his eyes, all the while choking. Mr. Okada turned red and elbowed his neighbour. It was several lessons later that I was to learn my commands were not suitable Japanese for adults.

My baby-talk commands were perfect, however, in a more important way. They endeared me to these people.

I was a learner, too, fumbling with their language and willing to take a risk.

With each class the decorum tumbled. In Japan, with old age there is not as much need to observe the stiff social conventions. The stops were out! As I walked in to greet my students weekly, I had the feeling that Mrs. Nakaguchi had instigated a plan to have a little fun with me in class. At a designated point in my contrived lesson, she would shuffle up, grab my flashcards with her withered hands, and impersonate me with her own bent frame, imitating my every gesture, all the while conducting the class in an uproarious English review. The Silver Club students responded to the cards as I heard my pitch and intonation coming from Mrs. Nakaguchi.

Normally I would feel inept at such a scene, but the mimicry was hilarious. I realized that my goal of teaching English was not necessarily shared as enthusiastically by my students. Their curriculum was not English; it was fun.

Some had never played cards before and I introduced the childhood card game, Fish, for the opportunity to practice requests and the 'do-verbs'. "Do you have any fives?" "Yes, I do. I have two fives." "May I have them, please?" Mrs. Ohashi began bringing her battery-operated card shuffler to ensure that Mr. Takeuchi could not keep any up his sleeve. However, once my back was turned, the insistence of all members to win the game would result in a swift shift into Japanese. My attempts to turn things back to English were initially futile.

A simple form of poker was another of their favourites. Each member of a group received a number card which was to be placed above his or her head in full view of all other members. The objective is to guess one's own number through the process of elimination. In an English class, you are to guess your own number **in**

English. Once the action began, though, there was little English in the game in the beginning, only shouts of "Roku desu!" (It's six!) "Ja nai!" (No!) Mrs. Kaneko told me that most of the members were getting together on the weekend to practice English card games.

The school which employed me was contracted to send teachers to the newspaper company classes for a period of four months, after which time, for variety, they usually sent in a replacement. The Silver Club members thought there might be a turnover, as there had been in the past, so they petitioned the organization to ensure that Carol-san would stay. They wanted the fun to continue.

When my Silver Club students came to the English class they entered a foreign country where the rules were unknown, and, if known, they were certainly to be broken. To extend the metaphor further, they were willing to overthrow the dictator if it met their needs. They made up their own rules. They had fun and played in ways they hadn't since their childhood.

To laugh and to be connected with other people is to be young again. Mr. Koyama tells me he now has Silver Club members as friends with whom he plays golf three times a week. He is more fit now than I remember him six years ago. He is part of things. He is with people who can laugh together.

Mr. Koyama prepared his commemorative speech in English; his delivery of it in my presence performs the ritual of commemoration. Together we commemorate together, we remember together. (Casey, 1987, p. 218) As a foreigner, I am a safe confidante with whom he can share his feelings of the past. From the distance of our two cultures, Mr. Koyama receives a broader perspective. He sees his life as a long continuum, his personal history with its decisive points and his passage into a new phase of life. He leaves the past behind, not forgetting it, but no longer controlled by his past hurt and rage. He sees himself renewed by the acceptance and friendships gained in his English class.

The importance of Mr. Koyama's past is not just an abstraction shared in a speech he shares with me; we experience it together as he tells it and we both partake in the solemnity of the commemorative mood. The ceremony allows him to remember the past, and bring it to a conclusion in order to free him to be in the present. (Bollnow, 1989, pp. 67-69)

Mr. Koyama's rehearsed speech turns to a spontaneous form of talk in broken English as he conveys his transition from one who grieves for the past to one who actively participates in the moment.

Mr. Koyama was able to be accepted into the group under the guise of learning a language, simple card playing. Practicing English became a communion with others, a way to accept himself—to be at home with himself and, at last, to share a home with others. He moves out of his isolation and rage and finds himself accepted into a new communion with other senior citizens who feel for his wasted years and anger. The festive mood of the English classes allows him to be young again. It is important to him that he share his transition with me, for, as the English teacher responsible for the tone of the classroom, I was, in part, a catalyst for his change. Mr. Koyama commemorates his past and celebrates his present and future.

The Silver Club students learned English in ways that resemble what would take place naturally at home with guests over a dining room table through laughter and conversation. Fun is the intangible joy of the classroom which enabled my students to behave in such a way that they could leave behind a past which paralyzed their spontaneity. Fun is the outer manifestation of an inner joy that allows us to embrace life and to be in the moment, and more importantly, to make connections with others. If spontaneous play contributes to the child's growth, then this growth holds true for Mr. Koyama also, as he is transformed by joy to a person who participates fully in the moment with others. Through laughter and fun, Mr. Koyama regains a sense of youth lost to him earlier. I am reminded of the value of laughter in children and I think these words apply equally to Mr. Koyama:

Wherever laughter freely erupts, there is breached the feeling of separation, of contrariness, of reluctance to participate. The child can do nothing else now but join in fellowship and communion. (Bollnow, 1989, p. 20)

Fun can transform us, both as teachers and students, so that we can touch each other in our everyday lives. Laughter allows us to be vulnerable, fully human and accessible to others. The joy that results from it permits us to be open to the possibilities of the present. Joy is a realization of what lies ready at hand and in ourselves. Through the sharing of laughter and fun, we celebrate being human. Like the children in my classroom, Mr. Koyama is restored by fun and laughter to live his life more fully and, thus, he celebrates this newfound joy in life in the company of others.

Home at Last

In my family, Christmas and Thanksgiving received cursory recognition; report card successes met with a grunt or a complaint about why the rest of the marks weren't A's. Even small successes weren't celebrated: no hugs or embraces for a painting or a picture. There was no welcome, no "strike up the band—she's home!" There were no rituals to commemorate the events. No birthday parties, as mine was on Christmas; not even a birthday cake, as Christmas cake predominated.

I began to think about celebrating my own successes and special moments when recently I picked up a copy of *I'm in Charge of Celebrations* by Byrd Baylor (1986). In the story, a desert-dwelling girl decides to take charge of the precious moments in her life and hold her own celebrations in their honor. To decide on one's own celebrations is an important part of the act of becoming. To celebrate oneself is to announce, "I am important!" After choosing the event to celebrate, the desert girl records the event and its date in a notebook. This is to make one's mark—to be at home in the world. The girl recognizes the celebration as one to remember forever because it makes her heart pound. A true celebration is a feeling, a mood, that creates the significance for a celebration of one's relationship to the world. In the desert, a common place occurrence, such as a whirlwind, is ignored by others, but the girl takes special joy in it, enough to make it her first recorded celebration.

This poem has significance for me as someone who continues to grow and mature and care for children. There are many moments to celebrate in the day-to-day lives of children, but they are only to be recognized when the conditions make it possible. When my ability to see and listen to the students is finely attuned enough to decipher the deeper meanings of their expressions, and hear below the surface of the words, the atmosphere is shaped. That atmosphere creates a space for the children to explore and be at home with others, enough that they see themselves as part of a larger home on earth. It all takes time though, with enough pauses in the day to step out of the maddening rush to listen, to touch, to feel and to think. Then, there is time to stop, listen and celebrate growth with the child who says, "Look, look what I made!"

As individuals, we cannot experience the joy of the celebration if we do not stop to feel a sense of communion with others. Writing my experiences has created for me a deeper sense of communion with others. To do so has meant that I expose myself for them to see. As a community of writers, we created a classroom of trust for each other which opened a home for dialogue between us that led to our growth.

To see my memories in print removes the 'sting' from them; to discuss the events from my childhood objectively allows me to see what took place from an adult perspective. From this vantage point I see my parents with their responsibilities at that time; they were people susceptible to making mistakes, but doing their best.

We are not static though. I shared these stories with my father and they have opened discussions between us that have led to tears, laughter and a deeper intimacy than we have known before. I have increased hope for change that can be brought about through examining my memories, if I look as hard as I did in this paper. I am more at home with myself and others now, more willing to be a vulnerable person than I was when I embarked upon writing my first story almost two years ago. The classroom stories mark my growth as a teacher and as a person. These situations and relationships are made possible only through the growing trust created between my students and me.

Beyond the family, the right classroom can provide opportunities for children to celebrate growth, to relate in a meaningful way to others; it can be a place for them to develop strong and deep ties that hold them together for a time. It can engender a sense of belonging which lasts for a school year or even longer, as in Bethany's case, in the first chapter. The classroom can develop a circle of trust which provides for an understanding of who we truly are.

But can this feeling of being at home in the classroom last beyond the school year? The class will never be the same grade again with the same students. The children will never be that age again, nor will they continue to share a common experience with each other. But there is an essence of home that can be created in the classroom, something which is conjured between teacher and children that provides a security for them that goes beyond the moment. I have realized that the differences in the sense of home and being at home between the ideal family home and the ideal classroom are of our making.

Bibliography

Agee, James. (1957). "Knoxville: Summer 1915." *A Death in the Family.* New York: Grosset & Dunlap.

Banks, Lynne Reid. (1980). *The Indian in the cupboard.* New York: Avon.

Baylor, Byrd. (1986). *I'm in Charge of Celebrations.* New York: Charles Scribner's Sons.

Beattie, Ann. (1989). *Picturing Will.* New York: Random House.

Bentley, Roy and Butler, Syd. (1988). *Lifewriting: Self-Exploration and Life Review Through Writing.* Dubuque, Iowa: Kendall/Hunt Publishing Company.

Bollnow, Otto F. (1961). "Lived-Space." *Philosophy Today.* 5, Spring 1961, pp. 31-39.

———. (1971). "Risk and Failure in Education." *Modern Philosophics Education.* ed. Strain, John Paul. New York: Random House.

———. (1982). "On Silence—Findings of Philosophico-Pedagogical Anthropology." *Universitas,* 1, pp. 41-47.

———. (1989). "Ceremonies and Festive Celebrations in the School." *Phenomenology + Pedagogy,* 7, pp. 64-76.

———. (1989). "The Pedagogical Atmosphere." *Phenomenology + Pedagogy,* 7, pp. 5-11.

———. (1989). "The Pedagogical Atmosphere: The Perspective of the Child." *Phenomenology + Pedagogy,* 7, pp. 12-36.

———. (1989). "The Pedagogical Atmosphere: The Perspective of the Educator." *Phenomenology + Pedagogy,* 7, pp. 37-63.

Casey, Edward S. (1987). *Remembering: A Phenomenological Study*. Bloomington and Indianapolis: Indiana University Press.

Coles, Robert. (1989). *The Call of Stories: Teaching and the Moral Imagination*. Boston: Houghton Mifflin Company.

Duerk, Judith. (1990). *Circle of Stones: Woman's Journey To Herself*. San Diego: Luramedia.

Heidegger, M. (1964). *Basic writings*. New York: Harper & Row.

Langeveld, M.J. (November 8,1974). "Personal Help For Children Growing Up." *W.B. Curry Lecture Papers*. University of Exeter.

Lathem, E.C. (Ed.). (1969). *The Poetry of Robert Frost*. New York: Henry Holt and Co.

Nin, Anais. "Letter to a Young Writer." *The Journals of Anais Nin*. (1976) ed. Genter Stuhlmann. Vol. 5, 1947-1955. London: Quartet Books.

Paley, Vivian Gussin. (1989). "Must Teachers Also Be Writers?" *Occasional Paper #13*, September, 1989. Center for the Study of Writing. University of California, Berkeley.

Peck, Robert Newton. (1974). *Soup*. New York: Dell Publishing.

Pienkowski, Jan. (1989). *Christmas, the King James Version*. New York: Knopf.

Robinson, Barbara. (1974). *The Best Christmas Pageant Ever*. New York: Harper & Row.

Rogers, Carl. (1969). *Freedom to Learn*. New York: Macmillan Publishing Company. Bell & Howell Company.

Rosen, Michael J. (1992). *Home. A Collaboration of Thirty Distinguished Authors and Illustrators of Children's Books to Aid the Homeless*. New York: Harper Collins Publishers.

Rosen, Michael. (1989). *Did I Hear You Write?* London, England: Andre Deutsch.

Rylant, Cynthia. (1985). *Every Living Thing*. New York, N.Y.: Macmillan Publishing Company.

———. (1991). *Appalachia: The Voices of Sleeping Birds*. San Diego: Harcourt Brace Jovanovich.

Schutz, A. (1964). "The stranger: An essay in social psychology." *Collected Papers II.: Studies in social theory*. The Hague: Martinus Nijhoff, pp. 91-105.

Shaw, Stephen. (1990). "Returning Home." *Phenomenology + Pedagogy*, 8, pp. 224-236.

Smith, Stephen, Montabello, S. and Zola, M. (1993). "Voices of Experience: Pedagogical Images and Teaching Practice." ed. Ricken, T. and Court, D. *Dilemmas in Educational Change*. Calgary, Alta.: Detselig Publishers.

Smucker, Barbara. (1990). *Incredible Jumbo*. Toronto, Ont.: Puffin Books.

Stone, Elizabeth. (1988). *Black Sheep and Kissing Cousins: How Our Family Stories Shape Us*. New York, N.Y.: Viking Penguin Inc.

Todd, Douglas. (Sunday, November 23, 1991). "Taoism: accepting life's flow in a hyperworld." The Saturday Review, *The Vancouver Sun*.

Vandenberg, Donald. (1975). "Openness: the pedagogic atmosphere." *The Philosophy of Open Education*. ed. David Nyberg. London: Routledge & Kegan Paul.

van Manen, Max. (1982). "Phenomenological Pedagogy." *Curriculum Inquiry, Ontario Institute for Studies in Education*, John Wiley & Sons, Inc. 12:3, pp. 283-299.

———. (1984). "Practicing Phenomenological Writing." *Phenomenology and Pedagogy*, 2, pp. 36-69.

———. (1986). *The Tone of Teaching*. Richmond Hill, Ont.: Scholastic Canada Ltd..

————. (1989). "By the light of anecdote." *Phenomenology and Pedagogy*, 7, pp. 232-253.

————. (1990). *Researching Lived Experience: Human Science For an Action-Sensitive Pedagogy.* London, Ont.: Althouse Press.

————. (1991). *The Tact of Teaching: The Meaning of Pedagogical Thoughtfulness.* Albany, N.Y.: SUNY Press.

Webster's seventh new collegiate dictionary. (1969). Toronto: Thomas Allen & Son.

Wilde, Oscar. (1989). *The Selfish Giant.* New York: Simon & Schuster.

Winning, Anne. (1990). "Homesickness." *Phenomenology + Pedagogy*, 8, pp. 245-257.

Index of Stories

Index